**Landscape
with Mutant**

**Landscape
with Mutant**

Frederick Pollack

Smokestack Books

1 Lake Terrace, Grewelthorpe, Ripon HG4 3BU
e-mail: info@smokestack-books.co.uk
www.smokestack-books.co.uk

Cover image: Front-cover:
Francis Picabia,
La Femme aux gants roses
(Woman with Pink Gloves),
also titled L'Homme aux gants,
ca. 1925-1926 oil on cardboard laminate;
41⅜″ × 29½″ (105.09 × 74.93 cm)
San Francisco Museum of Modern Art,
Fractional gift from Jan Shrem and Maria Manetti Shrem
© Artists Rights Society (ARS), New York / ADAGP, Paris.
Photograph: Katherine Du Tiel

ISBN 9780995767577

Smokestack Books
is represented
by Inpress Ltd

for Phylis

'The highbrow and refined pursuits of the OBERIU poets, their search for thought on the edge of meaning, were realized at the cost of their lives, carried away by the meaningless and entirely inexplicable Great Terror. At the cost of their lives, the OBERIU poets inadvertently proved that their basic sensation of meaninglessness and alogism was correct: they had felt the nerve of their epoch. Thus art rose to the level of history. Participation in the making of history always exacts an unbearable toll on an individual, but it is this participation that harbours the kernel of human existence: to be paupers but to enrich many, to have nothing but to own everything.'

NadezhdaTolokonnikova
(from her final statement to the
court at the trial of Pussy Riot,
Moscow, August 8, 2012)

'su cuerpo dejará, no su cuidado;
serán ceniza, mas tendrá sentido;
polvo serán, mas polvo enamorado.'

Quevedo

Contents

Sad Café	11
Oboe Sonata	12
October 2016	14
Election Eve 2016	15
'Children of the Future Age'	16
On the Beach	17
Day Eight of Trump	19
Liaison	20
Sign of Saturn	22
The Cry	24
The Airship	25
The Regime	26
Oath of the Horatii	27
Christmas 2016	29
The Lamp Bearers	31
'Surface Streets'	32
Apollo	33
Scandal	34
Garden of Theophrastus	35
Landscape with Mutant	36
What Flowers are at My Feet	37
The Hit Man	43
Rough Guide	44
Black Op	45
Alternate Poem for Obama's Second Inaugural	46
There There	48
Gentle Breeze	52
Cold Dead Hands	53
Be That Way	54
Romney at CPAC	57
Dreams of Nothing	59
I Want to Perpetuate these Nymphs	65
The Uses of the Past	67
Prosperity	68
Godzilla	69

Forward and Back	70
For P., ill	71
Get Ahead	72
Secret Handshake	73
From a Footnote	75
Day Trip	76
How It Works	77
Marginal Note	78
Neighbour, Eighties	79
The Week's Fools	80
Masters	82
The Inspector	88
That Being Said	90
Graveyard in Pottsville	91
With Thanks	93
Riddle of the Sands	94
Latest Place	96
How Embarrassing for You	97
Helicon	98
Elitist, Motel 6	99
The Colours of the Roofs	101
Public Domain	103
Dwellers Within the Walls	104
Go-to Guy	111
Ode to Cereals	112
The Just Judges	113
The End of Brangelina	114
Ripped from the Headlines	115
Results May Vary	116
Gnome Note	121
The Companions	122
'And Hearts that We Broke Long Ago'	124
Recognition	125
Let Us Hear from You	126
The Upper Terrace	127
Boxed Set	129
The Print	130
Sobornost	132

Tulum	133
Tough Crowd	135
Bear with Flag	136
Kin	137
The Sect	138
Opus Posthumous	147
The Cold Dancer	148
Touch	149
Flight	150
The Shadow Knows	151
Gudrun	152
Running Lights	154
Note to Cavafy	156
Crag	157
Two Views of Escape	158
Beatus	160
Aglaea	161
N.J.	163
Why the Classics	164
Non Omnis	165
B-movie	166
North Shore	167
Strange to Think	168
Bad Hair Day	169
Romance of the Form	170
Romance of the Pen	172
Expedition	174
So to Speak	175
Afternoon	177
Hoot	178
Huge	180

Sad Café

Shortly after the fall of communism,
I wandered through a populous city
with the first of the new guidebooks.
The café was as advertised:
framed caricatures from the former era
of writers and artists who had hung out there.
I wondered what bureau had decided
the subjects and parameters of distortion.

Service was nominal, sullen, a kind of theatre,
or desperately friendly – I forget.
Two older guys talked, softly, clandestinely,
whether out of need or habit.
It wasn't clear if their obvious
dislike of me was financial (with which
I could sympathize), or some nationalist-racist
thing whose time was coming but not yet.

One dude, perhaps a philosophy prof, was thinking,
perhaps, that he should go into advertising,
then remembered that he opposed advertising
and returned to the *Ding-an-sich* and cutbacks.
A woman, possibly pioneering, entered;
her clothes epitomized the dowdiness
of the rest. But she alone smiled, knowing
that from now on no outfit would be adequate.

I took out my notebook and wrote
the future. Flies buzzed. Flypaper
had been removed as hopelessly démodé.
Outside a homeless man, a member
of the new International, knocked and
sank to the ground beside the window,
uttering those obscure remarks which,
if listened to, would not have to be made.

Oboe Sonata

1

My calmest most sequential thoughts involve
the End. Fundamentalists, plague.
Jellyfish, algae.
Millions of tons of methane released from tundra.
Leopardi in his notebooks
remarked that such reflections comfort old men.

In '82 I knew a German girl.
I was a tourist fling, she was a symbol.
Preternaturally beautiful
and a mean drunk, she used to look at my books
and growl, 'Why do you care
about so many things? I care about *nothing*.'

2

In Roman times, Sparta survived,
barely, on tourism. Young aristos
on the Grand Tour rode down from Corinth,
complained of the bad wine and flea-ridden inns.

They watched some sort of communal dance
in which degenerate heirs
of the hoplites mimicked the endless spear-
and phalanx-drill of the old days.

The high point, apparently,
was a bloody beating and caning
of youths, who bore it impassively,
and of slaves representing the ancient serfs, the helots,

who were expected to cry.

3

When I teach, I feel a suspect ease
that also comes when I mention teaching
in poems. I have *five* kids this term.
The department should have cancelled the class
but hasn't, and goes on paying me
my smidgen. We meet in a room
with no chalk, broken blinds,
and an amazingly skewed chair
in a corner. Outside, the new Science Centre
goes on being noisily built,
an institutional whimsy: they can't afford
to hire famous faculty for it,
however much they raise tuition.

One of my girls has read *Great Expectations*.
A boy, an ex-jock, thinks he started it.
The black kid, son of a preacher,
alone gets biblical references.
None of them knows any history.
I've long since had to learn to distinguish knowledge
from brains and pitch to the latter.

The course is Poetry Writing.
The black boy yearns
for some fiery unclear apotheosis.
The girl who read Dickens has always wanted
to *hold* a book of her own; in high school
she copied and bound her 'very angsty' work.
The jock has some horror in his past.
The other two, both girls, take frenzied notes.
They all feel sorry for themselves and sometimes for others.

October 2016

Even a civilian may escape death many times,
remembering them over
the photo of a veteran with transplanted
arms (not legs, unfortunately); and
another, of Venezuelan schizophrenics
curled on a dirty floor and chairs.

But supplies of feeling (perhaps stalled
for lack of appropriations
in some private contractor's warehouse) are
replaced by the nullity
familiar to those who serve and those who don't
who have avoided pain.

The schizophrenics (the paper says) are mostly
aware they're mad and that they need
drugs which are now unaffordable;
those who survive
will soon no longer know this, only that
they're thirsty.

And the soldier, new hands limp
on an oddly arranged blanket, smiles
at the attractive fiancée
beside him; and she smiles,
inspirationally, hopefully, because
what else can you do?

Election Eve, 2016

A million miles away, at the next table,
a boy weaves, his expression
bored but controlled (nice kid).
The mother, mildly lined, seems *there*,
easily coping. The sister
looks farther off, perhaps at the orbit of Mars.
Two old guys, heirs
of the café wits of Paris and Vienna
as this Barnes & Noble Starbucks in Bethesda
is the simulacrum of a café,
read. But those are distant stars.
By the window, a youth guards a stack
of car-, a girl of fashion-magazines
as if they were the empire of Alexander.
A black guy taps at his laptop
as if each keystroke launched an empire.
We are the professional classes;
we keep our hands and much else to ourselves.

All liberals here. When galaxies merge,
individual stars almost never collide. The real threat
is subtler, in the most intimate layer
of space-time. At any moment,
an instability could tear apart
everything, down to the individual protons, leaving
not even a healing, eventually formative gas.
After years of work, Woodmont Avenue
has crossed Bethesda Boulevard to connect
with Wisconsin. At the intersection,
Paul's, Passion Fin, Pottery Barn
preside, the first two with outside tables.
Above them new condos with five-meter ceilings
rise and gleam. They are really quite beautiful,
might even subsist in some form
in a just society.

'Children of the Future Age'

are another species. Hierarchical,
still, but not intensely; the scene
is all very live-and-let-live
until, briefly, it isn't.
At every level they remember (i.e,
retell, constantly, proudly,
the myth) that they
or something like them once ruled.
(One could recall what someone said
of Hungarians, that no one works
because everyone's family is noble.)
Still, they're deeply emotional.
If a visitor from the past
(though not that mythical past)
comes, perhaps flees
to them, they inspect,
comment, commiserate. But their sympathy
only goes so far, never as far
as questions or action; and at the least
untoward gesture
they all fly back into the trees.

On the Beach

For a moment before we revert
to impersonal savagery, our expressions
are the curious gentle tolerant
love-hungry mistrustful
norms of our prior world. They comport,
more or less, with the nirvana
of the musclemen and the girls in thong bikinis,
the joy of the ageless skateboarding Sufi,
the warmth of the sellers of shades
and T-shirts, the smashed wisdom
of the man who each day re-sculpts
a nude from wet sand. One might suppose
we and they are the vivid personalities,
marginal whether flourishing
or drowning, and so now all here
at the margin. But there are so many of us,
suddenly, beneath that all-forgiving
yet merciless sky! One would have to be
in one of the topmost condos
of One Hundred Wilshire, two miles north,
to count! And the souvenir kiosks,
racks of terrible art,
masseurs and astrologers are being
however inadvertently knocked down,
the great nude trampled. Is it
a biker or tweaker or disorientated
suburban liberal from the other coast
who throws the first punch? The weak
exist to be trodden, and those who are trodden
are weak. There's no time
to wonder what armed line
forbids us every direction
but west, into sand, beyond
the overturned lifeguard platforms, towards

the ineradicable smell
of effluent, and
the sea,
now looming past the corner of one's eye.

Day Eight of Trump

The outer boughs are cartoon red,
the core still pale green.
Red leaves cover the slope
as if they will be endlessly replenished,
and there are three such trees along Whitehaven.
The others, normal for a hot (the hottest)
summer, dully turned dull brown
a month or more ago. But the wind
is properly coolish, the sky full
of small, quick, doodled clouds.

This street is schools, now letting out.
The Catholic kids, in their uniforms,
somewhat repressed; the seculars
(in layers of cotton, still, not down),
bouncing. The girls in their pinks and greens,
especially: two twirling
around their clasped hands, one skipping.
(So skipping still exists!) The boys
already, comparatively, lumber,
and seem, whether alone or grouped, to take in little.

I'm in no hurry, Mayakovsky wrote,
yet shot himself an hour later.
And Brecht in exile, watching a leaf fall:
Tricky to calculate that leaf's course.
Though not its destination.
Rush-hour begins, ever earlier; the cars
along Macarthur hopefully alert
for children, speed traps, and the forecast rain.
You can be certain you're an enemy.
It's your choice whether also to be a threat.

Liaison

I knew from the start that I bored them.
Of course they were more than polite,
with that silence which is a promise
of all the time you want to fill.
Not fishing for thanks or wonder,
they cured all age-related ailments,
returned my hair and my mid-twenties
while listening to the story of my era,
which predictably became my story.
Yet I sensed they'd heard it many times.
Grew certain when a door opened –
they still have doors – and behind it
were row on row of flashing lights
(miniaturize, compound, repeat).
Which struck me as the least one could expect.

Endlessly tactful, even loving,
a certain pedantry the only vice:
statesmen whose names I should have known;
the exact dates of extinctions.
Though relentless white seemed right for them,
they knew the value of bright colours,
surprising textures, rare and precious wood.

And their manners, primarily a patience
that became meditative
when strained! There was neither the big grin
a critic of my day called the great flaw
of utopias, nor ideologizing;
only a moment of stiff choice
before spontaneity. Someone long past
had pried the guns from all the cold dead fingers,
melted them down, and now
a discipline as hard as their ceramics
ruled in the domes and the far-flung oases.

I could live alone if I wanted.
I would live quietly in any case.
There were cults of stars, the past, and motherhood;
none would be pressed on me, but as I gazed
at the pale calm eyes, born old, the brief kind smiles,
I thought how neither they nor I,
across ten thousand years, was fooled.

Sign of Saturn

1

It was a mistake to tell a friend
I'm 'basically a timid person.'
Such confessions are harmless
when in youth you're trying on selves,
but not as grave clothes.
Tossed into the street,
I search in dumpsters for a blanket
to keep me warm, at least, until,
in the absence of pills and shots,
death claims me, hopefully quickly.
When this dream becomes intolerable,
I take public transportation
to Transition Headquarters. The street
is impassible, not only because
of Secret Service and mercs,
but history, which is reluctant to observe
this embarrassing moment
before the race war and the droughts and floods.
In the chaos, however, I manage to meet
the noted antisemite
who is now Chief Strategist.
I tell him I'm weak, want to surrender
and, instead of going through the well-known
stages of degradation,
wish to be sent directly to the camps.
He says they're not up yet,
I should wait a few months.
Or I could go to the Reagan Building
where neo-nazis are meeting.
The stubbled jowls split wide:
'It may be less official than you'd like,
but I'm sure they'll take you out back.'
'I thought they said,' I mumble,
'they're just doing it for the lulz.'
'Lulz,' he says, dismissing me,
'are the only reason we do anything.'

2
In the middle distance,
a gouache of my wife's:
a squat ceramic Mesoamerican
pitcher, blue with pink and salmon flowers,
a cup of the same pattern over the spout,
background twilight sepia.
How unsanitary, I thought typically
when I first saw it –
one cup… Beside it on the wall
a melancholy rural scene,
flight of crows, by a friend
with an abusive husband.

Though it's only mid-morning, I've set aside
my books and am drawing
on already existing
material – not memories
but an unwritten, barely even thought,
critique,
like the dark matter around galaxies.
It's trying to assert itself, write itself,
in letters of fog on darkness,
replace all the books in the house,
and even my journals and quarterlies.
Political despair can do this
if one listens
to the wisdom of actual masses:
The most salient question about people
is whether they can hurt you, how, and how much.

The Cry

It shouldn't be surprising
that one of the first invokers
of 'TRUMP!' as statement
of principle and threat –
in this as in other cases
to a Starbucks barista
who wasn't fast or white enough
(though possibly whiter
than her comparatively moneyed
accuser), and whom he
also, therefore,
loudly and often
called 'bitch' –

was not a member of the working
or quasi-working classes
that voted for greatness
(and will never be forgiven),
but one of the suit-men,
with doubtless loyal children,
relationships of some sort,
perhaps at one point one
of us, but who
could at last strike a blow
for his father hate and his mother pain
and his true love sleep and his friend cocaine.

The Airship

It isn't made for surveillance, but it's what
we have. Flying just above
the highest of the drones: the candy-coloured
delivery demons, the bland ones spying
for the other side. We are so much
the opposite of a stealthed
craft that we're counting on
the stupidity of domestic radar
to ignore us. Meanwhile we gather
whatever data we can (whatever good
it may do) about attitudes
below – the new nocturnal
tooth-grinding generally reported
by dentists, the rising tide
of bile that will crash triumphantly
on no shore. And are meanwhile strangely lulled,
despite our terror, by the homely smell
of gas and us and rubber, and the burr
of the engines at quarter-speed. Those below
(they are all, of course, lovingly armed)
could shoot us out of the sky,
so we installed mirrored panels
on the underside of bag and cabin;
when, nudged by shadow, our enemies
look up, they see and admire
only themselves, as they would anyway.
No one but they could wish such a fate
on us or this machine! We should
be coasting, ineluctable breast and phallus,
above the skyscrapers, near the sun,
buoyed by hope and awe, the sound
of our motors like old cheers from an old recording.

The Regime

The philosophers have adjourned
for the day.
They have left me the donuts
they didn't eat.
(Philosophers' love of donuts
exceeds that of policemen.)
I see two glazed, half a bear-claw,
as partial payment
for my keeping them in work; but this
may be an inversion
of the real situation.
I sweep crumbs, oil
(on schedule) the long table,
vacuum. Through the glass wall,
sunset enters
the dark wall monitor.
Secrets within the latter
could be useful to someone,
but I know no passwords,
and the philosophers don't need them.
Far below, a man runs,
another has collapsed;
which is better, God knows.
I vacuum then draw
the sumptuous curtains.
They're the colour that Trakl
associated with childhood,
Vallejo with iron,
and I with the long
ride home, avoiding
muggings, reflection,
the bars, and Immigration.

Oath of the Horatii

The first brother sighs
against the somber columned background:
'Our family, the enemy's, and
the towns they rule are equally
undemocratic and corrupt. If I thought
we were championing anything
worthwhile, I'd be totally
up for this, but as it is…'

The second brother, struggling to appear
to belong in his armor and not
to whine, says, 'I never
imagined I'd have to volunteer.
Neither did the shrink I've been seeing
to try to get painkillers
legally, and for help cutting down…
He thinks it's an imposition.'

The third brother hides, as much as he can,
behind the stalwart limbs and greaves
of the others. 'At least you guys
are buff – I could barely fit into this.
I've let myself go
since the Academy. I can't
get dates, and often I want to just
sleep the day away, despite the dreams.'

And the father, holding up the swords, with
one hand in an attitude
of invocation, mutters: 'These things
are heavy. So are the beard,
the posture and look, and this obsolete role.'
But the sister married to an enemy,
off to the right
with the wife who is the sister of an enemy,

says, 'If you don't step up,
they'll say that all that expensive
education and therapy and
lifestyle creates only pussies, and they'll
be right. Moreover,
we'll be worse off than if you die.'
The brothers, seeing the justice of her plea,
reach for the swords and pose heroically.

Christmas 2016

We do what Jews do: movie, Chinese food.
The film is one that all the reviews
called good or great, and my wife's friends
have seen, and I owe her a chickflick.
But after ten minutes I'm carefully still,
not looking at my watch. Someone's unfaithful,
someone cries; a dog runs into woods
at the edge of an impossibly nice park.
A grandma advertises all her progressive
attitudes, a kid acts out.
There's a black friend, and an Inner City
like a fever dream. I think
of how the rending metal and explosions
of orbital battle in *Rogue One* could
be justified, though there's no sound in space,
as being heard *inside* the doomed warships.
I think about feelings, and how many senses
can be ignored. I wait.
Our usual place is closed; perhaps
they took to heart the big point
the President-Elect is making
at his rallies of wishing his supporters
'Merry Christmas,' not 'Happy Holidays.'
They're great survivors, the Chinese.
We're not such great survivors.
We find another place. My wife
discusses the film, though she admits
it wasn't good. Outside
it's cold and everything, of course, is closed,
but surprising crowds enjoy
the lights. They're not all Jews or Moslems.
Some have that look I've noticed all my life:
a pro forma softening, a performance
of good will that would not withstand
the least bump. But this is

a liberal town: there's a menorah
in front of the bookstore, one of the last
of the last chain; one could feel,
if one tried, at one with the land,
fresh air, complimentary sentiment,
and sixty million fools.

The Lamp Bearers

At least it was secular.
I wouldn't have to stand, sit, stand,
and endlessly praise
something I deny and despise.
I wondered if, in a better, rational,
mildly collectivist society
(whose arrival I also doubt),
ceremony would exist without
boredom, religious holdovers,
humanistic bromides.
I advance this question not,
unpoetically, as argument,
but as what, step by step,
I thought; part of the ritual.

They stood, not with torches,
sooty and difficult, or candles
(flame has its own undoubted pneuma),
but faux-antique, dim, iron-framed
electric lamps. Their outfits
and expressions weren't fancy;
nobody *beamed* at me, and nothing smelled.
Under a moderately vast
dome, a voice
without charisma or embarrassment,
'sincere' for what that's worth, exact,
which is worth everything,
and mildly urgent, praised something.
I told myself it was me.

'Surface Streets'

I forget where I drove, or stopped,
in the famous city. But retail
is retail, and every speed-wired
salesgirl or counterman, seeing me pass
during long afternoons in the red,
knew an equivalent shop
in the next fifty miles of shops,
perhaps with better parking, would get me.
Under that palm-streaked sky.
As well as some diner, TGIF, or Red Lobster,
for food is the infinite.
Chains yearn towards each other
from the multiple centres,
retreating only when they meet
zones where regretted people
periodically burn their regrets and retail.
Under that dodgy sky.
Certainly I didn't stop
only to shop. Love superimposed
points on the map, where curtains rose
in the wind from window units,
dust hovered in sunbeams, heart-rates fell,
and I had to be going.
Then there were parties, under
the matte and cloudless night,
where everyone worked at nothing,
saying without speech or thinking,
*We're human beings, we have feelings and roles;
we hate your eyes.* And if asked
I would have apologized
for my eyes, but had become what I beheld.

Apollo

I have these few gifts left. For lovers,
gardens and cottages, self-contained,
inviolable and lovely amidst
ruin. Yet always
the he of each pair
immediately apprehends
boredom. She likewise
seeks in my faded eyes
a better deal, adventure elsewhere,
but finds only kindness.

Scholars and artists get,
besides my validation,
libraries, studios,
with unproblematic
support-systems; bars,
cafés on the corner with Wifi
connection to Olympus. Why then
that gaze from their windows,
as if missing the knock
of the thug, the fanatic?

I shrug and ascend
to my temple, pillared,
timeless in style, admittedly
staid. All around is a wonderful
parkland of sorts, with big tattooed types
knifing each other. They justify this
as culling the weak, not noticing
that they die too; that the weak
are therefore all gone,
or that there is no end of them.

Scandal

In another world, I pulled the plug
of the Great Mainframe. What can I say?
I was young and clumsy.
By the time we got home, home
was looted and our civilization crumbling.
But it was always doing that. 'I'm surprised,'
said Mom, 'that this cycle lasted
this long.' No one mourned, for we
believed, one and all, in taking responsibility,
healing, not looking back, turning blood
into blood sausage. And died
of heat, thirst, spells, and scavenged blades
in the sure and certain hope
of heavens we spent our whole lives
inventing. (One could say
we were all immensely creative, without art.)
My several fathers fell to small-arms fire,
Mom to something we ate.
By the light of burning cities, I preached
that *I alone was responsible*
for the troubles, and that they *were* troubles, worth
complaining about; and was loved,
like any entertaining heretic. However
(and I should have foreseen this), orthodoxy
returned with greater joy, and for my sins
I was condemned to your life,
to 'poetry,' to this pointless superfluity
of wavelengths, these few and graceless limbs.

Garden of Theophrastus

This week in the greenhouse:
a man who, seeing conflict,
proclaims both sides intemperate
and blinkered, so he can be virtuous and inert.
The wife of a plutocrat
who must portray her husband
as one of the poor in spirit, rich in feeling.
A casual electronic wrecker
of lives who, when cornered,
excused himself with Asperger's.

Souls are sumptuous and poisonous.
They like to think of themselves
as machines, but are only plants.
Their leaves extend like salutes, sticky
tendrils dangle, colours warn and seduce.
They breathe their own air.
If they were mobile, they would have to pull
plastic bags over their heads.

I keep the temperature stable, water
and talk to them. Their little scraping voices
talk back. Each sees
itself as the protagonist
of an unwritten or a mysterious, immanent
novel. Prose, however,
is only mulch.
I tell them this and they turn insulting.
Accuse me of not admitting I'm lying there with them.

Landscape with Mutant

Comfort would require hundreds of trillions
of dollars, a will of titanium, organizational
élan, exploding even
the most slumberous volcanoes
(to absorb sunlight),vast linked screens
in orbit (same reason), and reducing,
hopefully by peaceful means,
the human population. Only then
could I sit in peace beneath my vine and fig tree
or weeping willow.

Under the grey still sky, I'd collate
my notes. The mutation doesn't know
it carries the future
in its genes; it only feels
like a freak, like one of the failures
littering the range. Any successful species
should preserve the solidarity of losers,
but losers have none. I have plans
for universal empathy and forgiveness
if I am allowed to breed.

What Flowers are at My Feet

1

As I walk among parenthetical crowds
on the wide and relatively whole
sidewalk, I am periodically elsewhere.
The condition doesn't affect the inner ear:
without slowing or stumbling
I observe an auditorium
where I also am, my lecture or reading
finished, taking questions from the crowd.
They have more and more questions:
the ramblers, speechmakers,
easily panicked and inappropriate
have yielded to the succinct, eager thoughtful;
and in any case I'm attentive, patient,
a mensch. The atmosphere is such
that a movement could start here,
a faith – but I'm back
in this world, on this street, looking
at luggage I no longer need
and never could afford, to calm myself.
Then in the next block I'm home,
Huge alternate home, the inner life
comfortably outsourced, the children
eager to leave, seeing a benign abstraction
when I enter, the wife
without compunction buying things online.
I have an appointment in our world
that I don't want to keep. Afterwards
the street is briefly empty, terminal;
scratching, coughing, armed, I push
a cart along it. But that episode
is easily analyzed as I gaze
at a boutique that sells only olive oil:
failure means nothing where everything
has failed, loneliness less if everyone

is dead. Amazingly I don't bump
into people, dream my way into traffic.
It's as if I walk other, diagonal
pavements up there. Or as if
a pair of feet descend and I am their step.

2

I look back fondly on the beaker
in which I was born. I remember purpose.
Hundreds of reverent Third World tour-groups
organized by the State Department
filed past. They had not yet begun
to express themselves: no one broke me,
no one yelled God is great
as a way of saying I wasn't. A Soviet researcher,
forever famished, doubtless a former *zek,*
strained at his leash to observe;
I felt an affinity. My developing eye
took them all in
through swirling amniotic crystal.
The people to whom I was issued
did their best. The parameters of the program
wavered: sometimes I was subject
to the pressure of other egos, sometimes
to the vacuum of freedom. It's no wonder
I dysfunctioned, that meetings were held,
budgets cut, careers on my behalf
ruined. Then there was only
television: those of my cohort
will remember licking and stroking screens
that lacked the tang of later media.
I'm sorry the lab is landfill, I'm sorry
if I was responsible. I miss my beaker.
Adolescence, call it that, involves turmoil;
hopefully future
subjects will be spared it, one way or another.

3
We needn't ask why Father Flotsky
in full clerical garb is crouching
trembling in a shaded dirty room.
Nor need we widen our viewpoint
to reveal more than a smear
of blood, nor ask if he's addressing
himself, the dead, or Jesus.
Like a recently convicted high-profile
sports pedophile, he maintains in some way
his innocence, asks
what else could be expected
from spawn of the ungrateful underclass.
What demands explanation
are the ectoplasmic female figures,
blue-shifted, continually
approaching without touching him.
Their smile seems inappropriate, not sad.
Being plural, and in other respects, they can't
be Mary. Their sound-track
is the liquid somewhat modal vocalise
that in movies denotes
a watching psychopath. Father Flotsky talks past,
talks around them,
his questions and categories those
of the Bronze Age, their antiquity
validating them in his mind.
He repeats them until he plays
every role, especially the most victimized,
in the room; and continues until
they all become meaningless, hiding
less fungible things. He feels degraded by
the filmy floating hallucinations. But they
continue to seek him, shedding neither
their garments nor their music to become
sirens.

4

In a brief moment after the system
throws you a bone, you accompany your wife shopping
and sit in a Husband Chair,
watching her vanish and reappear
among the racks. She smiles ruefully
back because what she's holding
won't fit, or she knows she'll hate and return it.
There are two other husbands, one uncool;
one, properly patient, young, stays close
to his superb blonde... they look
as if they'll go home and make love.
In this town they're probably liberals,
but something in his jaw
reminds you how, the night after the election,
with friends at a restaurant, you raised
a toast to Obama; and how someone
three tables down yelled 'Fuck Obama!';
and of the face you saw,
briefly, exchanging death-eyes.
– She's taking a while, trying things on.
Fine. You read; check your watch,
but only about a pill; consider
how in a poem the second person
should only be used to mean anyone,
not 'I.' Especially not when I
is the poet. Why pretend
your experience is comparable to anyone's,
that someone will identify with it?
It's like the pretense of democracy,
of latent or emergent reason, good-heartedness,
egalitarianism etc.
one buys into every four years, repressing
the knowledge it will promptly be betrayed
But oh, election night
was good! And the week since.
They should be immortalized somehow.
The Republicans are gibbering, frothing, in fugue-state,

praying. One of the trolls
on Salon wrote 'Fuck all you idiot asshole
socialist faggot babykiller pagans,'
which you thoroughly enjoyed:
the purity. And you wonder,
Could a poetics be based
on reciprocal hatred? A steel point
of self-definition, erasing Yeats'
distinction between the 'quarrel with others' (rhetoric)
and the 'quarrel with oneself' (poetry) –
'completing' (Yeats, again) 'one's partial mind'?
Probably not… The sun
through the plate glass, and the overheated store,
have made you drowsy. You awaken
to see your wife approaching
with a big bag and a sweet look
of concern. Muddled, you struggle up,
think There are no more errands…
we'll go home and make dinner.

5

What is standing on me? asks
the earth. No it doesn't. Earth
absorbs ignores comprehends
the digging claws of a dog or squirrel,
bottles, condoms, the threat posed
by metal-detectors. Flowers meanwhile rest
in neat beds behind wire, grateful
for signs identifying them and trees,
for language and Linnaean classification.
Operating through dogs, grass trees and flowers
reach out and bond with the young
throwing frisbees, even sunning themselves
this warm fall. And the buildings beyond the park
stand straight like trees, with stylish curves
like plants and glass like air. They gleam
in the westering sun, at dusk disgorge
theatre goers. The hottest tickets

ask whether understanding, justice,
other grand things are postmodernly possible
and answer, thoughtfully, yes. So do
the shows at all the museums, open late
tonight with free admission. Or else
the elegant people from the towers
are descending into the night to help
people in parts of the city still
dark from the great flood. Which
apologized, like sharks, like mildew
and viruses: they can't help themselves,
and this is understood. Through the crystalline air
a wave and particle of love
radiates like memes, sticks like thistles
across the gentle city. We don't live there.

The Hit Man

Lacking the pride of the predator
and the warmth of the herd, they have only
an unconscious wriggle,
a glance the quality of whose absence
varies. As usual I had outstayed

my welcome, and paid, and left.
Yet I love the regularity of buses,
the slope beneath the Catholic school
precisely cleared of leaves – all those tasks
rewarded not with hunger and the whip,

only with boredom. At dusk
fog settles, which may prove useful later,
and a certain loneliness that won't.
Fortunately, however,
it isn't the task of thought to hit the target.

Rough Guide

Those whom the gods destroy go mad
in one of two ways. Some decide
they're right about everything and can do
anything. Which leads
quickly to disaster and termination,
or at best a long sentence of,
at best, apologizing. The others
also decide they're right but not right in a way
that anyone will ever understand
or accept, and that they can do nothing.
You see them in the back rows
of movies, picking up the week's groceries
at 7/11, appearing, however little
time they are actually there, to hang
around schoolyards. Mostly you don't see them.
If you engaged them
in conversation, though why should you, you'd find
they agree with the most advanced thought
that truth is entirely conventional, a social construct.

Black Op

It was during an interrogation
that I realized they might win.
He was so amazingly stupid,
you see. Computer skills,
weapons training, four
languages orbiting
a barren rock
of prayers and slogans. More than just
that love of death, it was
the fact they had so small
a step to descend towards it.
An ant dies; ants win.

His remaining eye
met mine, and I saw
our women in bags, me prostrating
myself, dust and crap
everywhere, bribe-taking epicene
cops. It was like
what liberals must feel,
crying out, helplessly entering
the vortex. But I'm no liberal.
He broke – not because of
our procedures, but because he saw
me too embrace fate.

Alternate Poem for Obama's Second Inaugural

Death is the mother of beauty.
Wallace Stevens

If you find yourself out of your comfort zone,
you may find yourself confronted
by someone who doesn't understand
the need, either for dialogue
or to defer gratification
of desire, resentment, or pride.
And if you try to explain
his error or your humanity
to that person, you'll appear
to believe you know something
he doesn't, that you have
superior knowledge, which
increases resentment.
Really you should have remained
in your neighbourhood, perhaps
abstractly sympathetic, gazing
as it were over the head
of the other until
his neighbourhood became gentrified,
his beliefs unfashionable,
and he or they went away.

Meanwhile you must understand
that beauty with its flash suppressor,
seductive grip and rate of fire
is not contemplative
but visceral, interactive;
that no amount of collateral
damage can devaluate
beauty. Any more
than burning cars
or brain damage minimize
the glamour of the race or game
that is their occasion and their frame.
Death is the mother of beauty; her
devotion will not end till beauty dies.

There There

1

The first stop after the Bay
is elevated. To the south,
the vast Main Post Office,
red lights on the roof, bright windows
squinting through concrete, trucks
jockeying. It heartened me.
To the north, old wooden structures, few streetlamps.
I once saw a naked woman
running across one of those streets,
pursued. A liquor store, solid
with mesh; this was before tough acrylics.
Two 'clubs' favored violets and reds;
I stared into their upper rooms.
This was before cellphones but
not boomboxes, carried on
sometimes by youths who bunched together,
laughed and glared; then I
was scared. Most of the people
who boarded at night, however,
were the late shift from the PO and the docks;
they sat heavily, silently. Then I was reassured,
and privately extended
(if I had room for it)
a standardized empathy.

2

At a place I liked to eat,
the local baseball star
had a breakfast named for him –
two pork chops, eggs, fries, waffles –and
his picture everywhere.
Splayed signature.
I could read undisturbed, watch the cars.
For a while there was a waitress,
in no way distinctive

(we smiled but never spoke)
except for a certain look, or something
only I saw: a point
on the far side of a hill
I had begun to climb. Not the tallest –
the one between anyone
and death – but real and, when I looked at her,
transparent. Unusually for those days
I never asked her out,
though she was still attractive
enough, and plainly alone.
But I had a sense, a glimpse
of myself at that table;
and thought how my father,
who had recently died, would never
have dressed as poorly, nor sat,
nor gazed as I did.

3

Once I went to a party,
I forget whose and where.
Bad idea.
A couple was slowly, nastily breaking up;
they were out of their minds.
A girl was out her mind for other reasons.
A guy I knew was very prematurely
impotent (this was before Viagra).
We weren't drinkers or druggies, at least
not yet. We sat drinking coffee,
talking crap, and eventually it was morning.
Someone had the idea that we should eat.
Barely able to think, we drove
to a place near campus, agreeing
to pay for what's-her-name who had no money –
this gave us purpose.
At the diner, entropy continued. We watched
the sun come in the windows,
showing streaks. I wondered

if I would ever leave,
go home, sleep through the day
on my solitary bed, be glad I had one…
It occurs to me
I could have cried into that apathy
that we were still young
(enough), that we should talk to each other
(relate to each other) differently, cast off the discontents
of competitive possessive
individualism, become new people.
It occurs to me now, but wouldn't have worked.

4

There was a street with stores
as prosperous as the comparatively
minor downturn of that era
allowed, and the local oligarchy
(devoted mainly to stability)
needed. One place closed
soon, but I think I went in
twice. Polish imports.
(This was still during communism.)
I wondered if the wolf-eyed ash-blonde
pani knew I was Jewish.
A four- or five-inch
glass figurine of a clown, striped like some blossoms,
limbs twisted/relaxed, the long head
declining from the long neck
to the thin chest, the expression
brooding beneath the paint, ironic/
silly beneath the brooding, etc. etc.
As I left that last time,
the sky may have streaked pink-gold
beyond the gentrified nabe, but sunsets
are not very interesting. I walked
a lot when I lived in that town, on both good
and chancy streets, and often now
retrace those steps in thought; they seem vaguely heroic.

5
And once, near the Art Museum (a striking
design, like a blockhouse
being reabsorbed by forest)…
But I'm losing the sense
of where things were. It may have been
a zone precious to power or merely
one where it stored necessities,
and paid people
to sweep. There's an appeal
that grows towards the end to streets
where no one walks but someone binds
and mulches the small trees. Between
hotels whose conferees
fly out the next day, immense
conspiratorial corporate
buildings and buildings
full of files, the Jail Annex, and –
seen from some point –
a ten-story windowless
half-square-block structure. Like,
I think now, a piece by Rachel Whiteread:
one of her plaster casts of empty rooms.

Gentle Breeze

I had great hopes of being nice
when I was young, but was variously balked.
Now dogs suspect me and make clear
they are only not biting to save
their pack, the real humans, from lawyers.
Nature-poets and flowers
wilt as I pass. Fonts boil in cathedrals
I tour. Birds enfold me
In their contempt (birds think
they are still dinosaurs and that they still reign,
however reduced). I add
to the massive depression of grass.
And liberals, though I'm on their side,
regard me with the not-thereness
they reserve for gun nuts, rednecks, victims
who misbehave and people who believe
there is no justice, only sides.

Cold Dead Hands

We good, smart, sensual, kindly, tolerant ones
are loath to admit we have enemies
though we know we do. And so we
think very little about them,
mock them in private, live carefully apart,
distance ourselves from them
if they are what we came from, visit
on holidays, abstractly mourn
the crankiness of families, the ubiquity
of cranks. We put our trust
in the law, which safeguards
distance, enforces
the higher impersonality that
is tolerance. But to our enemies
law is a clown mask, tolerance
the farce around the mask, violence
passion, and nothing earns more passion
than what they do not want to understand.
Therefore, for their sake and ours,
in the name of that intelligence
and social love on which we pride ourselves,
we should learn hate by identifying
what in ourselves does not want
whatever we believe, however wrong,
to be traduced, or anything we have,
however illusory, to be taken.
And wait in long lines to buy guns.

Be That Way

1

Aged five, he was told to stop feeling sorry
for himself. His mental jaw dropped.
Despite intolerable provocation?
And more importantly, what else was there
to feel? Is not the human soul
integral, like a tree, or, better,
the cycle of water? He could have cited
Kierkegaard: 'Purity of heart is to will one thing.'
They told him not to be smart.
Worst was the prospect
of an impassive visage, the self-policed
self-distanced mind reflecting
the grainy light of injustice, i.e.
causality, forever. Which in the event
he wore, eventually discovering
compassion, which is in large part
a feeling of superiority
towards people who don't have it. And received
the resentful secret knowledge
of his part of the world, comparable
to fetishes elsewhere: total misogyny,
death-worship, vendetta.

2

A wrinkled street of smelly bungalows.
A closed park in a bankrupt state.
Apartment buildings barely blocking
snow. Sidewalks whose vanishing point
was desert. Fellow renters sentiment
proclaimed free of viciousness but full
of pathos. They won't be contained
in complete sentences; they are sentenced.
No longer symbols of another world,
they are a memory that they were symbols.

Frosted sliding doors
multiply as the mind
awards itself a pension, but through them
the ideal remains visible.
I mean a sudden inexplicable
outbreak of pity, analogous
to the Big Rip that will end things;
the past reformed;
a general descent from the cross.
It doesn't matter if you understand this.
Understanding begins in mystery and ends there.

3

One day the Road Runner, hurtling past
(full speed alone is speed), saw his foe,
the Coyote, lying at the lip of an arroyo.
The fleet fowl checked (it took infinitesimal time)
for some new trap designed to fail –
an anvil from the clear sky, spring-
loaded cliffs, acid sand,
a strangely mobile hole –
and prepared to evade, mock, and leave.
(Language for him was generally
confined to one phrase
of will and indifference.) But he saw only the Coyote.
Who, always lean, looked starved now,
and mangy. The eyes –
heretofore restricted to an aped
cunning, triumphalism, or a despair
as white as desert sun –
seemed fixed on something past the sun,
jaws wasting their last moisture on a smile.
Whatever trick this was was not crude,
so couldn't be the Coyote's. The Road Runner
approached. 'It wasn't hunger,'
wheezed his enemy. 'Stringy thing
like you wouldn't fill me.
It was the pointlessness

of your running around. At first I just wanted to ask
where you're going. Then it drove me nuts.
I guess it's speed
that makes you smart. I almost had you
a few times. Now I've found someplace
where I'm fast enough
and won't be hungry and my plans will work.'
'Can I get you anything?' asked the bird,
bending to him. But the Coyote
apparently saw no further point in talking.
Omitting his cry, the Road Runner
after a moment sped away,
wondering if he'd miss the Coyote –
the challenge. Probably not;
challenge to him was neither here nor there.
And, vaguely, whether he and the Coyote
were or had been halves of one thing. No.

Romney at CPAC

Before I enter history (whose work
is that of an intern, vaguely patronized),
I want to say I'm sorry
for disappointing you, and to express what I've learned.
I thought that in my tense delivery,
its desperation so impacted
for so long that it seems, to me,
ease, you would recognize
a shared yearning of the soul: to hold
the foe down, then praise oneself for hurting him
as much as necessary but less than one could.
Admittedly my jokes, etc.,
failed; but isn't every attempt
to be a regular guy, a white man,
just that, an attempt? Requiring lenience
from those who somehow benefit from it?

I would have spoken had I been allowed,
until my voice was gone, about my faith.
It's like yours, but more so. To the Father, Son,
and other free-weights of the mind, it adds
a lurid epic, and a peculiarly resolute
denial of death. Trained thus,
I could espouse wholeheartedly whatever
you wished, kiss unborn babies, eat your food.
Because faith, I thought, was faith: your faith
that you in essence are as rich as I
though temporarily embarrassed; the faith
we share, that the wealth
of one is that of all; and mine,
that the barbed wire around factories
I buy in China is there for safety.
Surely, I felt, my faith had earned some slack.

But finally we let each other down.
A parody resents a parody
of itself, as well as the real thing.
Black fascist muslim communist jewish
bankers on welfare are coming
for your guns and other talismans of freedom;
you knew this but I didn't. Or rather
I do, but we both know I'm safe from them,
and so they don't exist for me
except as a convenience, like yourselves.
I wish you leaders who can feel your fear.
With them you may, as Kafka once foresaw,
march arm-in-arm, invincible, reclaiming
the cities from the unproductive, singing
full-throatedly while at each other's throats.
For man is a wolf to man, but howls in chorus.

Dreams of Nothing

1

The rent is paid, which has the status
of a miracle, self-wrought, his alone;
or an escape, however brief.
He draws the shades, so that in time
he will imagine a day
cleaner than those in time,
and sits feigning peace until he feels it.
Then paces. Each rigorous step
redeems something, carefully thought,
comprehensively mourned,
till hurt can be no longer itemized;
and only featureless pity
is left to go where needed,
hope without content
to join the hoard already made.
A thumb, two fingers at right angles
mean that he grieves for everything in space.
Two palms extended
signify the Friend he seeks to be.
Pointless to mention the squalor,
the closeness of the air:
they are a token of their opposites.
Or the extraneous judgments
that, toward nightfall,
accumulate like street noise, like
clouds, like
cramp in the hours hunched beside a wall.

2
A sphere arrives. Its genteel form
manifests intellect, the fact
of deceleration power.
These things combined
could cause panic. But say
They don't want to cause panic
or other idle talk; are hardly a 'they'
or thing, but a focused slice of space
nuzzling our orbit like a cat.
Their former chitin, limbs, or feelers
long subsumed in thought,
with perhaps a nostalgia for bodies
and evolution like a misspent youth,
they transmit waves of tentative, so tentative
love. They only want to locate,
and do, good. Reason for them
is warmth. They are as tactful as gravitons.
But now they turn and flee faster than light,
sensing religion.

3
In the mid-1930s, a Futurist –
aging, no longer mad
for 'the slap, the box on the ear,
the speeding motorcar more beautiful
than the Venus de Milo!' (Marinetti),
or, at least personally, for war –
sculpted plants. From tin,
enameled fuchsia, azure, aqua,
crimson, violet, gold and white.
Spiky, some bordered, striped, they stood or hung.
They were neat. They looked
like stylish microorganisms grown
imperial. *I raffinati*, if not
the *bel mondo*, all wanted one.
After several shows and the Biennale,
they went into museums. The sculptor

had long surrendered
his youthful faith that the museums should be bombed.
Pondering his heroic garden,
but disconsolately passing
Sironi's reliefs of peasants, soldiers, mothers
(*he* should have had that job!), he followed
crowds to a plaza
where Mussolini was endorsing
Romanness. Though he joined the chants and cheers,
the sculptor savored
the texture of the crowd (like a three-day beard)
set off by banners and the black
of priests and party, the Duce
like a jerking muscle, faces
gleaming as they rose to watch
a flyover of Breda fighter-bombers.

4

Sometimes the supreme imaginative object
for me is a critic, posed against
an indeterminate bleak background
like a conference room at Area 51.
Who stares at me in horror
or mild disdain. I've never quite grasped
our grounds of dispute – my indifference
to sunsets, rural life, traditional form, simple
sensuous diction, pop lyrics, sports,
the oppressiveness
of syntax, the importance
of Derrida, Spicer, childhood, graceful en-
jambment, the endless pathos of parents, the theme
of love, the need to avoid
allusions to academic controversies, the vital
insights of 'other' sexualities and The Other
generally, the impossibility of confrontations
like this. I'm not even sure
of the other's gender – it may be Helen
Vendler or Marjorie Perloff (see footnotes),

though I doubt either would be caught
dead in that dress. As always I
respond by yelling *IT'S ALL ROCK AND ROLL*
and as always realize too late
that what I yelled was an aporia:
was it praise of, a claim on, certain subject-matter,
or rejection of it? Meanwhile the figure before me
is losing shape, in response to my rage or
its own or sneakily to remind me
that a poet's job is universal empathy
and identification. I almost soften, reach out; then think
that people in the humanities
deserve no mercy anyway. And look
past him or her to what I can see,
beyond the conference room,
of a field of flying saucers crashed at various times
since Roswell, and yearn to get out there –
though whether to repair one and go home
or weep in the shade of its exotic metal,
I don't know. In either case, despite
my leftist sympathies, I'm about
to pull a John Galt (see footnotes)
and tell the swine to get out of my way.

5

The recent death of a girl
I lived with forty years ago
is revealed by an idle Google-search.
Unspecified illness. Two years younger. –
One must distinguish
emotions that can be named and are felt
from those that are named (with a dying fall,
say, beige bravery, mauve irony)
but not felt, and those that can't be named
or aren't felt. The names and feelings
coexist like elements of a rainy day
in spring on a rainy day
in fall, or like those of life,

on Mars. My shrink, who is some years older,
is in the hospital; his wife had to call
to cancel. He is also between
the era when bourgeois Americans
casually and hopefully
admitted to having shrinks and now,
when once again they don't.
Several people I barely knew
died lately. It is of you
the rumour is told, the one that draws nearer and nearer.
We had no idea of a future
when we were together.
According to the Internet,
she did some worthwhile humanitarian work
later.

6

The window of a toy store. The old man
was surprised kids still touched
things besides screens and keyboards.
Among the ranks of dolls, like an impossibly packed
choir, was one with one huge eye,
red in green plush, and fangs
on each side of a wide embroidered grin.
It seemed a friend. He remembered
the dolls of childhood boys abandon soon
and won't admit to owning. His –
several – had been
a squadron, headquarters a card-table,
a bear his Number One. They had devastated
hostile planets and fleets with earnest
professional banter and the crude
technology of the times.
Now he imagined what he could have done
with the kindly monster in the window,
an alien come over to our side.
To combat bathos he summoned
a painting, John Hrehov's 'Collector' – an effete

hard-eyed young man in an expensive suit,
about to move or crush
a row of figurines
(an astronaut, the Creature from the Black
Lagoon, a soldier, a mummy)
on a rich surface in the coldest light.
And the doll said: If you think he
or anything is God, you're lost.
The manipulator
is also on the table, and no taller than you.

7

And he went on, or I did; or the dude
in section1 went crazier,
and started hearing things
or saying them. But because he was saying them–
i.e., aloud – he no longer made
grandiose claims
for himself. A kind of blob
or area of space (he said)
is drawing closer. Not to Earth per se,
just the general area. But from even
a moderate distance, it appears to be
next door, on top of us, us.
It lends a shadow to the lover's face,
the kind of shadow you both fear and seek
when a woman stares from her thoughts and doesn't speak
or a man stops excusing and explaining.
It amplifies each trace of DNA
that has long lain unpunished or unredressed
in streets and alleys, darker yet
intolerably bright in the new darkness.
It has no name that can be grasped
by those who love and study it, or those
well-paid to obfuscate it, whom
it will inevitably eat. It dreams all things;
will, turning in sleep, transpose
what will be with what never was.

I Want to Perpetuate these Nymphs

Ces nymphes, je les veux perpétuer.
Mallarmé

They're playing in water. I register
noise first, and think –
you can't *get* more politically correct
than this – of Third World women,
friendly and briefly unoppressed,
washing clothes in some sewer.
Then the spray sinks and shrieking stops
and I realize the river is really clean,
there are no clothes anywhere, and
they aren't women exactly –

too healthy, gorgeous, fearless, and
immortal. And I'm afraid –
partly because of the Diana myth,
partly because it's a group,
however nude, of strangers. Also it's hard
to maintain eye contact
with those considering eyes, leaving
aside the other stuff there is to look at.
So I smile, think of making
some gesture, decide against it,

and the splashing, chatter and grabassing
resume. If I were
the Faun, I think, six-pack abs
above the fleece, not taking no
for an answer because he needn't ask,
spinning the world from the tune he plays
on his flute, the ultimate pantheistic
Bad Boy, they'd take me seriously.
Or were I, say, Alberich,
material dwarf,

vindictive cosmic loser, they'd take
me comically but at least interact –
I could *make* something of resentment.
Instead I'm just a nice American,
strangest of archetypes, a dollar short,
always ready to go
nowhere. It occurs to me
I might have crossed the river, moved among them,
if I'd remembered to be spontaneous…
But even in Arcadia there's ego.

The Uses of the Past

His English is impossibly good. His gaze,
like mine, seeks resemblance.
His posture is that of a tailor
who thought for a while he could sit
upright on a tractor, move large –
the sixth or seventh Jew in North Dakota…
His back remembers that.
And he remembers failure, Chicago,
but without the sighing and acceptance
I feared; rather my own proud, urban,
one might even say principled
cynicism. I apologize
for never tracking him down.
He shrugs. 'Why should you have?'
I invite reminiscences. 'Farming
is necessary,' he smiles, 'but necessity
is no recommendation.'
I express regret for projecting
on him my indifference to family,
tradition, but he says,
'I was after all a freethinker';
then in Yiddish, something about the future.
We talk freely all night except
about one issue, perhaps irrelevant.
His hand on mine in farewell
is so gnarled, with dirt in the palm, other
dirt under the nails, that I'm sorry –
despite the *Schwärmerei* – for troubling one
who died so many years before I was born.

Prosperity

One day I brought the kid.
He was a hit.
In his abstracted way,
even the boss seemed kindly.
The girls (of course I mean
the female temps) made much of him
(the kid I mean.)
Flirted, I'd have to say.
How elegant Reception
and corner offices,
how lively everything appeared that day.
Shelves of coloured binders,
crap on desks,
and items pinned to cubicles seemed
eager to play.

Several of my colleagues sat
him down before a screen.
'It's like a video game,'
they said, trying to explain
how the red line stood for quotas,
the green for quotas met;
then advanced the frame
for district breakdowns.
But his hands took the keyboard
(or was it the other way?),
small fingers clicking
to Graph, then up to Menu,
down to Programs;
his eyes were brightly focused
and he didn't respond to his name.

Godzilla

The belief that his approach
is entirely negative hurts him.
If the naysayers would only *engage*
with him, he could cite Action Painting,
Happenings, the whole vitalist-expressivist
current. Would admit
that his quest for the numinous,
self-contained act coincides
with a search for food, space,
a mate – but would then draw himself
to his full height and say, And your point is…?
People running or crushed under his feet
distress him, but he considers
how ruins are always a suggestive trope
and might someday create a responsive critical
climate. He broods more, as he works,
about how his ambiguities
of origin (radioactive waste?
pollution?), properly understood,
might connect with his audience, the screamers,
the soldiers – their great secret theme,
too, is Innocence. And sometimes he voices
the cry of any outsider talent:
Look for what's *in* my work instead of what isn't!

Forward and Back

Unable to accept either time or eternity,
I attribute my occasional rages
to eras of torture, dagger- and swordplay,
vendetta, and (because the human world
poses no limit) the usual roarings and rendings
of the Jurassic. My sweeter moments
derive from a halcyon uncompetitive
future that may not be on this planet
or involve any current species. Otherwise
I share the neurotic discipline
of monks and coral, the fearfulness
of the approaching millennial tyranny
of Superman. The self, you see, is a spooky
action at a distance impelled
by distances. The concept would be clearer
if I drank or you did,
for being fucked up is a timeless state,
the substrate of effort. Meanwhile I try
to make these Alexandrian or
late-Martian insights accessible
to students – not the fleeting,
intangible ones I see each day,
but you, my receptive Hittites.

For P., ill

I promise I won't say what's wrong.
You're always intensely private.
And in the era of Facebook,
Twitter, Youtube and the rest,
affirming Epicurus'
'Live hidden' may be the best
role for the poet.

I can't pray – it isn't cost-effective –
but cling to my old secularism
and secular hopes,
though in the present instance they don't matter.
Feeling hurt myself,
I find myself wondering how one could hurt
everyone. It seems unfair
that only the top .001
% can do that.

I'd kill them all if it would make you better.

Get Ahead

Before he opens his eyes
he knows the glycol has been drained,
that his brain's OK, an upscale body
grown from, grafted onto,
cloned for, or by some other
vivacious new technology attached to it.
In a moment he'll wiggle fingers
and worry about his shlong, but for now
it's all good. Sense of self precedes self.
There's a feeling of gratitude to money,
even awe: it went on paying.
Others thawed and spoiled but he
remained the favorite-flavoured popsicle.
Then there appears, not a doubt,
but a twinge of warming self:
what if they have their own agenda
and I have to pay more?
Perhaps they're disembodied wimps
who need someone to make the hard decisions:
which dome or slum-continent
to empty – use aerosols, bombs –
well, I'll be happy to consult…
Then a real worry: what if there's no need?
What if they only want to talk,
to ask questions… Almost he senses
obnoxious shrink-like beings a foot away,
and fights not to open his eyes.

Secret Handshake

What am I doing here?
They're all movers and shakers.
I'm not even a novelist
made meaningful by sales and a movie.
Should I approach that former Secretary
of Whatever, toss wine, yell 'war criminal,'
which would accomplish exactly
as much as not doing it,
plus a painful, Fed-assisted exit?
Why did they (did they?) invite me?
Young women and some buffed and botoxed
back to youth and joy centre
clusters of lawyers, traders, spooks,
while others grip and steer
jowls. Is that why I'm here,
to empathize and thereby humanize
this slice of the ruling class?
One's bored without empathy.

I recognize another poet
of the sort they *should* invite:
future Laureate,
refuses to give up transcendence, meter, the theme
of Mother. Would an ideological-stylistic
set-to between us
edify them, like the string quartet in a corner?
And is that why…? I head towards the drapes,
the heavy embroidered drapes, to push them aside
and peer out. But am waylaid

by a General,
medals and build of cliché, eyes of a courtier,
who proceeds to tell me
with logorrheic bonhomie
unspeakable things. I'm ten times over
exposed, doomed to redaction or a cell
in a Supermax. (With at the same time a store
of images to last successive terms…)
When, just before
the guards set down their trays
of hors-d'oeuvres to take me, I ask
my new friend why. He grins:
'Poetry
is the continuation of politics by other means.'

From a Footnote

Because he was taken
and released (for no reason) early,
the others in the communal flat think he's lucky
and leave him alone. Anyway, he has nothing
to steal. A table
two meters from a window
(but his sight remains good). Pens.
His pince-nez.
He learned in the camp to censor
unhelpful senses. Smell – forty adults
and infants in the apartment.
Hearing – tears, beatings,
drunks, the trials
of Trotskyite spies and wreckers,
interviews with workers
baying for their death. Mostly he's at a library.

He follows the early Nietzsche, whom he views
as a prophet, in opposition
to the later Nietzsche. The Dionysian
principle points away from
the basic, the Satanic Western error –
the self – towards joyful oneness in the God-man,
Christ. The Apollonianism
of later Nietzsche tends towards
the Man-god worshipped
by Stalin. But worship is worship.
One day the Cathedral of the Savior
will rise again, and the Bolsheviks,
having done God's work
in chastising and annulling
the self, will kneel, themselves annulled and chastised,
on its steps. Bells will ring
across the holy earth, and all will join
in something like an immense peasant wedding.

Day Trip

The strange stars and bombastic moon
of this toe of the world have set.
With impenetrable sunblock
and a wide musty hat, I look
for shells, those would-be fossils.
The *jefe* says such cloudless days,
as well as letting in the solar wind,
mean hell to come: roof-tin,
old pickups and the last few boats
perversely, convulsively embracing.
Soon the settlement will drown.
Bones of a glacier wink from the near peaks.
But tonight I'll lie with the widow
who keeps the hotel. Her beauty
quasi-deliberately wasted here,
she has made and heard every excuse,
accepts them all and believes none.

Over cards, awaiting the storm, I feel
as often through the years the comfort
of amicable independent monologues.
The *jefe* says that, even during
the dictatorship, it was left to him
to decide who was subversive, whom to shoot;
and that now, with privatization, it's clear
how authority is indistinguishable
from panic. The widow
says all the various stories
men tell are very quickly laughable,
transparent, but it's hard,
earns nothing but blows,
to prove at every moment one isn't fooled.
My hand is poor; my share is to explain
how the basic plots, 'you go on a journey'
and 'a stranger comes to town,' are obviously one.

How It Works

In eternity, victims
are splayed over the land,
and people spread over them
like ants on roadkill.
Some, encountering unappetizing
velcro or heels, fall indifferently back;
no harm to them means no foul.
Others attempt pity –
exude, that is, the digestive juice of pity,
and another that says pity isn't important:
what matters is the help that should have come
but didn't. From these bitter chemicals
plus part of what they eat
they prepare a golden nutriment
to be fed to their secret queen;
which, if they fail to deliver it,
poisons them. Other people, however,
perhaps most, say of the victim,
He is not dead, he only sleeps
and may at any moment rise to attack us.
They spear the victim with their mandibles,
which become hypertrophic,
which interferes with the ability
to digest. This enrages them further
but also exhausts them,
which ensures that this subspecies
spends half its life in sleep and half in hate.

Marginal Note

At different times I saw three friends despair.
One because of a condition.
One cheated on and left by the only girl
he had found confidence to love.
The third had reasons both broader and narrower:
that day in his kitchen he interrupted himself
to note with cold disgust
how petty and prissy and limited and fearful
he had become. There were others –
I think of them now – and those were only guys.
Women in my experience despair
more quietly, more rationally one might say;
they investigate, doubt, take their time.
These incidents occurred when I lived
in bad neighbourhoods in the shadow
of the hills or towers of the upper classes.
Hopefully those last allusions
get economics and gender out of the way;
not because they're not determinative,
but because when things happened
I saw no larger context
and couldn't think of anything to say.
It would feel better to adopt
another's pain, to howl and tear one's flesh
like a primitive, then babble magic advice:
Look in the mirror until you're someone else.

Neighbour, Eighties

The one time we talked, she said
she believed this world is unreal,
a corrupt version of another.
She compared it to a subway platform
downtown, gummy and dark,
with a little air from someplace.
She didn't proclaim this –
not aggressively, or as a cry
for help, or to have any effect –
but neither did she doubt it.

Long gone, no doubt. She was older.
I'd like to think I didn't
mention Plato, reiterable
energy-states, or any
of my usual abstractions.
Remembering her I imagine,
as a kind of offering, vast
jeweled vaults, a spectacular
yet intimate light, a sweetness beyond incense,
but they're all so second-hand.

The Week's Fools

The first, at a party, to my
'I kept my head down in high school,'
tinkled, 'I was popular,
did thousands of hours of volunteering,
played football, aced exams.'
When I said, 'Alienation
grew more severe in my twenties
but I wasn't really suicidal,'
the response was 'Everything went fine
until the Recession. But I was prepared for that.'
Covertly thinking another minute,
I came up with, 'It would be sad –
wouldn't it? – if an ambitious man,
especially in an intellectual field,
found himself on the Galapagos
with only iguanas to impress.'

Next day, a sensitive-superior type,
all breathy ethics, equated
Fox and MSNBC, i.e.
abuse and bias right and left,
to the greater glory of apathy.
And a religious oil-gland
oozed that my denial of God
showed that I really care about Him,
and the hostility of my reaction
that I can't in fact do without Him.
In each case I had a response –
would presently have delivered it –
but these people are protected;
a sudden ray of boredom
stills my voice and shrouds them.

Then over the weekend, I can't say why
or by what medium, a singer,
the greatest singer in the world this season,
attended by Beatles grandparents
with nasal cannulae and hip-hop grandkids
waving lighters, glowsticks, hand-horns,
squeezed love, lost love, mad love, neurotic love,
relics of agapé and Fate itself
into a tiny universe of art;
that music my enemy from the start.

Masters

1

One of my neighbours on that wing
became famous, inadvertently
and without benefit to himself.
His work was hung in museums
of 'outsider art' and '*art brut*' – terms
that would have offended and pained him,
though the doctors were pleased.
While he lived, we often discussed
the spiritual efficacy,
across the many worlds
he proclaimed, of his echoed line,
minute crosshatching, spired palaces,
and ranks of moonfaced angels looking on.
One of the latter died
whenever my friend masturbated – a great sin,
tallied by crossed-out eyes. When, near the end,
he was troubled by illness and rumours of fame,
the drawing was weak and there were many dead angels.

I was one of his pallbearers,
stood by the graveside, threw earth,
then returned to my station
in the hallway, by the entrance, near the table
on which every third day the sisters
placed fresh flowers.
There I sat with the Zurich papers, reading
about the Crash, the Nazis, the second war,
the atomic and hydrogen bombs, the moon landings
and cantonal politics,
avoiding my room till nightfall.
Some of the doctors as they passed
thanked me for my service,
the sisters less often. It's rare

and good to find, in any country,
an institution so enlightened
as to recognize the art of the insane
or the need for a flower-guard. With visitors, though,
I had bad moments
when at first they didn't see me as a patient.

2

Although well-known and respected
by 1934, Isabel Bishop
continued to depend
on a wealthy relation. That year she married Harold Wolff,
a noted neurologist.
He was highly supportive, to use a term
and imputed feeling that didn't yet
exist; insisting, for example,
that she return to work
as soon as their son was born, work being her painting.

He also insisted,
whenever they entertained, on formal dress.
Conversation was free
over drinks – the Old Fashioneds and Manhattans
he liked. Dinner was silent
except for recordings of Hindemith and Mozart.
After-dinner talk concerned
topics Dr. Wolff considered important,
and which (some people recall)
he listed in advance on 3X5 cards.
It lasted precisely two hours,
after which guests were politely asked to leave.

An expert on brainwashing, he died
in Washington in '62, debriefing
the U2 pilot Francis Gary Powers.
(They knew something was wrong when Dr. Wolff
failed to appear exactly at eight.)
In her studio overlooking Union Square,

his widow continued to paint,
with unrivaled technique and penetration,
women talking, women eating hotdogs,
women reading, men sleeping with
their heads on the shoulders of women
on benches in the park, the communities
of bums in the park, men and women
walking, erect, purposeful, equal,
in undefined spaces.

3

Long before the Hoods,
the ambiguous vector
of their whips, French fries morphing
into cigarettes and brushes, severed heads
(all single bloodshot eye) up against
bottles, the tangled-leg-creatures,
the hell-screen and the final triumphant spiders, long
before his daughter's memoir
of his self-absorption, even before
the breakthrough works of warring contemplative
boys, Phil Guston,
teaching in Iowa, entered 'a time of dismantling.'
The WPA was winding down
and with it his patience for murals. He wanted
to return to the easel, the even light
and transcendent gaze of Piero.
Some work from this time, however,
has been called sentimental. In *Sunday Morning*
a young black man sits
smoking, tie knotted, cuffs straight,
expression unwelcoming,
an Iowa City out of de Chirico,
empty and gold, beyond the window.
Nature comprises the abalone-shell
ashtray and the cheap wood of the table.
He is not Renaissance-timeless.
Perhaps he's wondering what it takes to be timeless.

4

The train was strafed but, by a miracle,
arrived at what was left
of Nuremberg; by another miracle,
a six-wheeler was waiting.
The driver, a corporal, gave his name,
which the painter promptly forgot. Hurrying
before the inevitable night raid,
they loaded the art. Some had to be abandoned –
jerrycans of petrol took up room –
and the painter charged the stationmaster
(who smiled at him oddly) with its care.
As they skirted craters and piles of rubble,
the painter mourned its loss.

The driver was gratifyingly familiar
with the work. He never stopped talking,
but at least he talked about the work
and was very respectful. He liked
the one of a girl getting screwed
by a swan ('You can see she's enjoying it')
and those of a guy having to choose
among three women ('I wish I was him!'),
though he wondered why none of them was blonde.
More sedately he praised the 'Party wives, I guess –
they look it – with all the flowers and thin dresses.'
'I forbid you to make of my work
a private pornography!' barked the painter
with a barrage of insults. Unfazed,
the driver said he admired
other things too, then asked why the pictures of farm-folk –
'German Soil', 'German Peasant' and so on –
never showed tractors.
The painter, momentarily at a loss,
suspecting then discounting
wit, answered in terms of essence.

At Küssbart the road was cratered. At Arschdorf
they hid from planes beneath trees.
At one point they thought they heard cannonfire
from both west and east.
Here and there, deserters and others
hung with signs on their chests. At Holzbein,
the SS at a checkpoint seemed
a bit crazy, but yielded
to the letter signed by Goebbels. Amazingly
they reached their destination. It was damaged,
but the cathedral complex wasn't.
Glad to be rid of this idiot,
the painter, nonetheless, stiffly,
shook hands. They both expressed faith in the *Endsieg*.
The truck drove off and, at the nearest crossroads,
turned towards the Americans. The painter

had to undergo
extensive questioning and offer sincere
excuses. The bishop found him a room
and food. The art from the truck
was stored in the cool ancient bombproof vaults
of the cathedral. When the painter died in the '80s,
for his local retrospective
three or four works were taken out and hung
amidst the stuff he did later:
Annunciations, saints,
Depositions in the style
of Simone Martini. One piece,
the first he had made in that town,
as a fleet of B-17s
flew past, very low, for hours:
crude, muddy and brown,
with the Four Horsemen of the Apocalypse
    each riding a fuselage – that one painting

                                              had quality.

5

Braque, *Guéridon*

The twisting ascent from the three
rusty feet, almost too small
for the weight of gifts on the table
they bear, is one of those gifts. A pipe
and a knife for the fruit are crossed,
six lines, a small device. The fruits
themselves allude to apples but also
peaches and waver towards firmness.
A glass suggests a bottle, a guitar
a face, two faces, the sheet of music words.
There may be flowers, there is certainly
wallpaper, walls of a sort infused
with space, sand from the beach in the paint;
somewhere out of harm's way
a subject watching an object watching
back, but mostly that third thing.

The Inspector

I have replaced the mosquitoes
with a slow, pensive moth,
which appears not to be drawn
to the lamp beside my cot,
but whose eyes reflect it from the dark.
I have kept, however, the mosquito-net.
As a symbol of sleep, it aids sleep,
and makes my silhouette,
if not attractive, more mysterious.

At dawn the clients gather on the steps
below the verandah. They point out
the unfortunate, colonialist
nuances of assembling thus,
and for that matter of verandahs.
They complain of confusion
about sex, anger, religion,
and what they perceive
as 'a sort of grey ticking'
in what they had seen as their minds.
We have lost authenticity,
they say, and cite as examples
that word, and the fact that they speak
in turn, without interrupting.

I reply, You will not always have me
with you; point at the mud
of their street, now clean and drying;
and gesture vaguely at the temperature,
which has decreased one degree
during my stay. The daily
moderate tremors show
they are moving towards Europe. Which, I console them,
has its own hands full,
must pull together now as glaciers advance.

By this point, the school day
has begun and boys and girls,
all in ironed whites,
pass, some hands linked. They should
be starting quantum computing
and critical theory soon, and show
a restrained but all-seeing,
all-dismissive confidence.
I do love children, whatever people think.

That Being Said

I started writing my memoirs when I was six.
Occasionally, plagued by the fetish
of subject-matter, I took time out
to do things. Suffering, enduring
required less investment.
Puberty and adolescence
disturbed the narrative and posed stylistic problems.
Events in a monk's cell
may be interesting; those in other types of cell
not. But trying to tell
yourself that the sort of cell
you're in is another sort – well, there's your story.

To defeat expectations,
I wrote as honestly and spared myself as little
as possible. Yet, sensing that exhaustive
Freud-inflected self-
indictment is another form
of grandstanding, I tended
from my twenties on towards lapidary moralism;
the test was if it made me cry. But by
my fifties I began to think,
It's society's voice
I'm channeling by writing thus,
not mine, not Truth's. So the judgment
remains suspended, though I've lived the sentence.

What remains to tell is that I wanted
a space station; my aunts bought me scarves.
They had no idea what a space station was.
Around that time I had a drum –
green; rubber, not plastic; it had a smell,
and a hand-painted Native American.
I beat and beat and beat the Native American.

Graveyard in Pottsville

When I get my degree I go to work
for a firm contracted to wreck
the planet and as much of nature
as possible on time and under budget.
My rise is swift. I have a nice place,
a company car, my own lab
and more and more people – great guys and gals,
all smart and dedicated – under me.

The firm bought most of a downsized town
and promised to hire locals.
But the locals, in their boarded shacks
and storefronts, are cannibal zombie tweakers.
Though armed, they seldom bother me
when, armed, I park and walk; which I like
to do, pleasantly melancholy.
It's an open-carry state.

In the cemetery, some graves
go back to the French-and-Indian War.
Even quite recent ones are nameless, dateless,
pale worn-down mossy stubs like rotted teeth.
(It must be the climate.)
Sometimes when I walk there, a horsefly or chigger
bites; as I slap, I think,
You'll get yours, fucker.

And the ghosts who accost me
in broad daylight are also highly
aggressive and pointed.
A girl who in the Twenties self-aborted.
A dude who made a pile
from black-market gas and nylons
during World War II, then ran afoul
of the Mob. His dad, a radical

deported during the Palmer Raids, but who
came back. They all have something to say,
one thing, offense intended though
I take none: Only the dead
are specific, individual.
The living (like me, for instance) all,
as far as the dead can see,
embody some superfluous abstraction.

With Thanks

Most of those who did the work
were on meds of some sort; those
who didn't, on downers and/or hung over.
Proportions varied. Neither group
liked her. She announced
tests, got them through tests,
ensured that no one (or only the fraction
the principal and administration
had decided was safe) failed.
When the cheery bong
that had replaced the industrial buzzer
sounded, she enjoyed the brief
stillness that followed
the out-rush, the occasional
forgotten pink or skulled and camo'd
backpack. Still, once or twice
each year, she tried
to tell them something, but had learned
never to reminisce. And each year
menarche and puberty
or something like them sifted lower and
the girls, even those who professed
to despise them, blew boys
who broke things and brought knives. Later,
few thought of her or voted for Hillary.

Riddle of the Sands

I thought the book I'd brought to the beach
would be interesting all afternoon.
Aphorisms by a newcomer
from a neocolony or some hole
in the wall in the metropole;
no one was sure. He styled himself
the Cosmopolite. His aim, he said,
was *non-mathematical, non-physical*
truths that would be recognized
by any intelligent species. If I'm wrong, and
my premises are too mammalian,
bipedal, etc, they will be
corrected in later editions
throughout space. If I may quote myself:
Life is an honest mistake.

The absurdity was obvious.
And yet these proto-thoughts
could be imagined under redder suns,
green clouds, beside a sea more poisonous
than ours; weird readers in
whatever fashion nodding at these insights,
till the collective mind,
however strict or muddled, intervened.
He assumed vanity and grief and wounds
(or rather that the universe assumes them),
but never war specifically – which
seemed cautious but made sense.
The day wore on. Beyond the limpid, hot,
gull-peopled sky lay dark,
and, everywhere in the dark, ambivalence.

Of course I can't endure much sun.
Sat under an awning, nursing (odd phrase)
a mojito. Walked, smeared
with sunblock. Found a stretch
of sand dollars and other shells
converting death to decorativeness.
There seemed a murmur in that patch of sand
beside that of the waves, and flies
on fish and seaweed which were merely dead.
Far offshore, dolphins leapt. I wondered,
was it high spirits or one of those gangs
they disillusioningly have
of teenaged males who commit gang rape?
They depressed me, as at last my reading had.

Meanwhile the other humans on the strand
were wrinkled, blobby, obsolete like me.
Full-flowing veins in a string bikini
seemed rare as mind among the stars; and yet
there are as many stars as grains of sand.
I longed for sunset on a world
that rotates once a year, and whose year is long.
I understood the language of the gulls:
they're rude.
Sometimes the Cosmopolite
dithered – it was his one excess –
over a maxim. *The particle
of irony is as ubiquitous and subtle
as that of gravity.* This eventually
congealed to *Irony is light.*

Latest Place

Muggers of a higher order –
thoroughly checked for hep, worms, STDs –
gather hours early
on either side of a gold carpet.
Security with its cattle prods
expels the uncertificated
and unruly, spooks paparazzi,
and glares civilians into passing swiftly.
When, in surrounding towers and along the marquee,
lights go on, the carpet seems
to writhe like a glowing beast in the depths of the sea
to welcome the first limo,
from which a power couple exits – she
wearing something amazing, he in a tux.
When they're halfway to the door,
a mugger (very strictly one)
breaks through the line. If he can get away
with wallet, watch or pocketbook,
he wins, and the place will award him
two months of leftovers or a year's worth
of vouchers for taco trucks.
However, krav maga, capoeira,
taekwondo are in fashion now
among the *jeunesse dorée*.
The slit in her long skirt isn't just for show;
nor are his bulging arms, nor even her heels.
When the member of the underclass
is down (she must be pulled from him),
the manager and goons raise a great shout,
the other contestants grumble. The two
customers are juiced; he gives a few bucks
to staff to carry in the bleeding mugger.
Then he and she enter to freshen up,
dance, watch a film or something
while dinner is prepared. It's a variation
on an old story: three went in;
two, obviously satisfied, come out.

How Embarrassing For You

I made a fool of myself.
Should be punished, but will escape.
The facts are classified – I classified them.
No cops thunder from pulpits.
No vicars park for hours near my house.
The papers, which say less and less
about anything, say nothing;
the talk shows, desperate for material
despite a glut of material, ignore me.
Lawyers circle, howl, depart, and fall on a deer.
Outside, the cold and overcast
are a trial, the coming hottest-ever
summer a verdict decided in advance.
Though people are gone because I avoid their eyes,
space itself is a cell,
and air and time the air and time in a cell.
On these walks I prepare, however,
if not a defense, a statement:
The world is composite.
It's made of shifting n-dimensional planes.
From a distance they look like motley.
Though I never wanted to hurt anyone,
they do. And really,
what, besides a fool, can one make of oneself?

Helicon

The poets welcome me.
They press a gilded wreath upon my brow.
Some wear togas, some spats,
some robes not cleaned for generations;
here and there an early-Soviet boilersuit.
My French is spotty, Latin nil.
The translations strike me as skimpy.
I marvel that they like my work,
without rhyme, gods, or hexameter;
'Don't get me wrong, I'm honoured' – But
they laugh. 'It isn't that,' says Tasso.
'It's the political situation
you've entered and are working in.
You're one of us now, negotiating
endless corruption, cruelty,
futility and arbitrariness.'
I notice Africans and a clutch
of minor mandarins, grinning.
'Not to mention the idiocy
of peasants,' says a Pole.
But someone else (Bossuet?) disapproves:
'You shall learn patience, natural order,
restraint.' Most of the others turn on him
and things degenerate; they all have tales
about nobles. 'One I was begging from
saw me once. He was at stool,
and ignored me even when I said, *Culo angelico*.'

Elitist, Motel 6

Night. The highway is a noise
both like and unlike the sea;
its red and white streams, in the aggregate,
a thought simultaneously
asserted and withdrawn. The darker
shadows beyond are hills, the lights
among them a hamlet of some sort,
if only trailers overpaying for stasis.
I focus on a glimmer to one side.
A comrade lives there. If we met
we wouldn't know each other, but
I salute the range and subtlety
of his or her contempt, he or she being
a constant, not a recurrent, fantasy.

I've been so busy lately... And
successful, in my way; the sheets
and towels are clean enough, the pillowcase
well-ironed, which makes up for
the absence of a green-wrapped chocolate mint.
Likewise a coke machine outside my door,
the television, all the televisions
working – who needs Veuve Clicquot
or company? Tomorrow it will still
be dark enough, when I leave,
to conceal what sort of town this is;
its pained, suspicious and resentful face,
now innocent in sleep,
waking in triumph as I drive away.

In the half-dark I wonder:
What was democracy for?
At last to have the deepest truest
image of the many
reflected in a gilded mirror
for them to follow over barriers
that turn, once crossed, to dust.
Though he slay me, yet will I trust in him;
though I enrich him, I do so gladly…
In the scrub woods behind this building, something
refreshingly unhuman coughs.
It left or has been banished from its pack
or burrow (explanations differ)
and has no other home than consciousness.

The Colours of the Roofs

I was young, but no longer young
enough. The room –
tiny, musty, mildewed, six
unaided flights up, whose bed
could discourage sex and banish sleep,
the last affordable in town –
possessed, through its narrow window,
a Corot view. The *albergatrice*
said, in her terrible English:
'You know that the sensitive young man
roaming alone and fateless with no aim
but experience through a foreign city,
producing only fantasies
and sighs, is less than a comic, is in fact
a negligible figure.'
'Unless,' I replied thoughtfully,
'his handsomeness and aura
make him, without effort on his part,
the fate of women, the cynosure
of geniuses in their café.'
Depositing the key on a scarred table,
she smiled: '*E non lo sei*.'

The sun gilded churches
and ruins. The haze
seemed less from all the little cars
than from history. I wouldn't unpack;
would wash, set out, see churches
and ruins. But for a moment
I tested the bed and stared at the three
fresh colours in the room: those of a knitted,
peasanty rug. I might watch this,
watch the light change;
get used to the smell, piss a few times
in the sink or down the hall;
save money (it was lire, still)
on museums, and mental wear and tear
on effortlessly elegant heedless girls.
Shape and be shaped by
a mood that quickly
scared me enough to drive me down
the six flights. For some reason
as I walked I remembered
the disturbing, still-recent image
of helicopters lifting from Saigon.

Public Domain

centenary of the Somme

Thirty years later, armies made
men climb from trenches, with rifle
and pack, and advance across deserts
towards somewhat distant A-bomb tests.
Most died of cancer
(they smoked to provide cover),
but the photos are stirring, archetypal.
Armies march on aesthetics.
Consider early sketches
of the tank, its frail but gallant adolescence,
the beveled beauty of the Tiger
and Panther, essentially handcrafted
(the artisan is brother to the peasant!),
against graceless Shermans
(Brooklyn as interpreted by Texas),
and T-34s crying Mother in every curve.
There is no real experiment in art.
Intuition is execution.
The insight of the Somme wasn't merely
the numbers of dead, but the response
of many men to weeks of shelling:
they gradually lost their names,
language and memory,
were left with various twitches, footage
of which can easily be found on Youtube.

Dwellers Within the Walls

1

The king is abducted from the midst
of his library. The cool vertical light
of his kingdom still rouses
the lofty leaded windows, but
he's gone. For years, in fact from the start
of his reign, his studies,
passionate, directed
by something subtler than reason, have worn down
this chair. Kings lived,
he reflects, first to kill and conquer;
then to cut ribbons
for projects lucrative to others; henceforth,
why should we not be the first and final
scholars of our realms? In gentle light
he meditates upon his nothingness
and that of human life, that of his subjects –
each, he is pleased to grasp,
the subject, himself a distant speck –
and a vast, pitying love
gilds the texts, illuminates
his notes, and binds him to his people in
his mind. The priests frown
at these insufficiently orthodox
researches. They are like rats
in the walls, scratching at thought.
He plans a salvation
vaster than theirs, less beset
by moving parts. The still chamber,
the confiding smell of heavy pages,
though borne away at once by the a/c,
promise at every moment an end of days.

And the ninjas strike. The king has time
to note that the black masks
and jammies that presumably annul
personality only announce it
more strongly. A chloroformed rag
edits time; awaking, tied to a chair
in a room too easily imagined,
the king is tirelessly shouted at.
Assumes at first some worthless branch
of the family or a clerical *fronde*
is fighting in the cause
of arrogance and indolence; then realizes
this violent band is acting in *his* name!
They loudly and repeatedly proclaim
love for His Majesty. Swear to behead themselves
for the shame of disturbing him!
But kings should not be philosophers.
(Thus the most stentorian
of the gang.) The roles
are antipodal. A king especially should never
entertain the concept Nothingness,
however arguably the basis
of human solidarity. Should renounce hope of the latter:
the folk don't want it;
they want simple, positive ideals, war, castles,
dynastic marriages, torture, jewels.
These ideas don't change the king's mind;
they have no logic; but the voices,
especially the chief's, the mere prolonged panicked
noise suggests a vision
more global and convincing than his own.
When he barks, they release him.
Loyal troops break in, arrest the loyal thugs.
At whose dreadful executions,
and thousands more, the king officiates
in long-abandoned ermine.

2

Mothers in that realm are famously what
they are not. Not rewarded
for their pains, except sometimes
with medals; not provided domestic help; not
listened to, though often self-doubt,
the weakness of seeing all sides, makes them
not want to be heard. The one who shakes her child
because it won't stop crying
knows what she is: in need
of sleep. Her classier sister knows
preeminently that she is not
that mother. Or is she? The image, the possibility
remain; self-doubt sustains them. A boy
ripens in silence, which he fills himself.
No distraught, improvised moralism
at school or elsewhere interrupts
his self-instruction,
which is focused by blows to the head;
he achieves manumission: a gun,
and maturity: shoots. He has many siblings,
who eat. Great placid balloons roam
the stores. They will not be shot
or, probably, molested; a long, kind, sickly
twilight has them in its care.
Around them labile hierarchies form.
Boys don't despise, they go directly
to hatred or, if possible,
disregard. Girls do what boys do,
more subtly and more often to
themselves. They observe
men, those acrobats whose five limbs flail
(the head, a sixth, is stunted); who break-dance and
do cartwheels, often wheeling
themselves away. High-ranking mothers
stare between calls on their time at plates
on which lie shreds of lettuce or,
as in the best cartoons, a single pill.

3
In that realm, in the capital
(which is most of it), between
the walls, Capital and Labour
celebrate the extinction of
their conflict, even of
their names. All now
are partners, and what they produce
is feeling. A worker
on the verge of being sent
to outer darkness weeps. A manager,
highly-trained, a specialist in
this area, bends
over the hunched form,
one arm across the shaking back (he's
prepared, however, for acting out),
and weeps too. So sad are the pressures,
so inhuman necessity.
They, employee and manager, could have
been friends. They are now,
in this extremity. The ex-worker
yearns toward the pathos in
the manager, is washed by his compassion,
transcends for a moment petty concerns,
sees the rightness.
The manager is genuinely moved.
The whole office or dying factory
is moved. He whispers in the worker's ear,
as a token of hope, the name of
a current enemy. Police also
weep when they must evict,
arrest or shoot somebody immature.
Executives, managers, stakeholders,
'partners' and beggars
round-dance in beery plazas
around bonfires highlighting
the enemy. Always, a general speaks.
To the extent career allows him,

he hints that walls and air- and cyber-
war will not suffice
for victory, but in his peroration hails
the king and assures the crowd
that victory is assured;
the face always shows,
despite the iron jaw, the slightly
epicene ambivalence of art.

4

In white, fluorescent-fitful, barely-
equipped faculty lounges or
dark book-lined chambers, scholars desert
the topics of their conferences, drift
insensibly toward what really,
necessarily, interests them:
the power of witches;
the means of identifying
warlocks (which any of them might be);
werewolves, hants, and
(e.g., among their students) succubi.
The tone at first is light, which passes
for rational, but soon devolves
on hushed authentic horror.
'I never thought it was under the bed.
It was in the closet.
And there *was* something in the closet.
But we moved, and I've never been back,
and that house burned, and now I'll never know.'
'And even if you'd looked, you wouldn't know;
whatever's there, however much pain
it inflicts, it isn't part of the world, has
no name, because language
(which we professionally overestimate)
is also part of the world.' 'One might apply that
to politics. Decay, betrayal – to see them
as merely an error in a system is
an error.' 'Could one say the same

about love?' 'Perhaps it's a privilege
to live in a closet.' 'You got that from Lecter –
I read it in one of his papers.'
'Did you ever notice his *hands*?'
(A shudder.) 'Like those of my ex-wife's
lawyer.' 'Like my mother's.'
'Like mine.' By now the torches have guttered,
and the general trembling
has grown to the point
that the scholars, nearly ghosts themselves,
are glad when a priest enters: Father
Something from the Divinity School.
Who gauges their demoralization
and sighs, but whose dismay
conceals perhaps a gleeful mental
hand-rubbing; one might even think…

5

An alarum from the walls, which all social
strata hurry to see,
texting or calling confusedly down
to those who cannot crowd onto
the battlements. What matters isn't
whether .50-calibers
or crossbows are being aimed, only the grim, timeless
soldier postures. What's primarily
shocking about the figure
outside and below is that it is
outside. Few come;
predictable rubes. The people
draw on that store of names,
images, fetishes which
are always there – more definite
the less defined, clearer when unexampled.
Is it a nomad
from tribes who suddenly exist
to the north and east, a stray,
a scout? Is it a barbarian

(he looks like a barbarian),
planning an attack? A leper.
A mutant spawned by tests
in the desert. A bad element.
But there are minds more curious and generous,
who imagine benign particulars and a general
welcome, so that they may be
disabused, and feel virtuous and martyred.
Perhaps he's a minstrel. He looks like
a minstrel. Squints up and back at them,
scratches his side, seems undecided whether
to caper, gesture obscenely, plead, or bow.

Go-to Guy

Two guys and a third. One of the two
is the sort of decaying blotchy heap
that currently means power;
the other visibly a lawyer,
who will (the waitress knows) subtly advise
the heap not to grab her ass, and pay
her off if he does. The third guy
requires an effort to notice, but it's
the two of them, and him, and,
between his undistinguished ears,
numbers. Somewhere a phone
awaits a call, a cubicle
the rearrangement of a wall, a desk
(soon to be cleared) an unsigned note,
the armchair in some country place
an artful masquerade
of suicide. She meets (she's young) his eyes
and sees, somehow not unexpectedly,
a vast forgiveness;
and, as she must, approaches
their bones and salads
to ask how everyone is doing.

Ode to Cereals

By the grace of hallowed dead,
unquestioning work, and our planes
and agents ever on watch, I will never –
to quote an old oath – be hungry again. Any
bike-ride under sketchy trees
in the new suburb is a drive in a new
car. Unexpected grace
descends, though the reassuring humdrum
remains, and there appear FROSTED FLAKES.

COUNT CHOCULA has the ahistorical,
timeless appeal of horror.
The brown of ancient stains, sublimed
by fresh arterial violet, spreads
as swiftly as electronics
from vaguely cellular platforms, bringing
adepts where they wish to go:
adolescence, the trans-parental realm;
and is the true milk of childhood.

Then, after the crazed mini-vampire
and all-accepting working-class
tiger, select spirits rally
to a pirate shorn of violence and the terror
of age: CAP'N CRUNCH. In his eyes
the glint of gold, the greed for it, are shared,
are generous. Gold is the special tang
in the taste, the spiky texture,
the dust at the bottom of the box.
Let there be no animadversions
about poison. With or without
blueberries, banana, satisfaction
follows the last or the last extra, 'heaping,'
spoonful, clicks like a tab;
it's a matter of digestion, of pacing,
and I lift my eyes to the clock.

The Just Judges

I'm given to understand
I might jump the queue
to recognition if I protest
Israeli settlements on the Left Bank.
(Mishearing the phrase thus, I form
an alarming but piquant vision of Paris.)
I'd have to sign something, boycott something.
Otherwise I could write an article
saying how inspired
I am by the power and authenticity
of hip-hop. 'Do they really want that?'
I ask. 'Wouldn't my approval
make it seem less… transgressive?'
The critic/prof/editor
advising me, a trans one could have a beer with,
shrugs over her beer
and gives me to understand
that neither these, nor gays nor feminists
(she ignores my protestations of support)
are the problem. Nor even my unfashionably
lucid, Horatian style.
'You don't belong. There could be a poet
rotting in an SRO
like Wieners, or in a nuthouse like Clare,
and he'd belong more than you.'

The End of Brangelina

She mentioned it briefly in class,
but some of her students wanted
to know how she felt, not what Foucault
or Judith Butler might have thought.
Well, I have to speak as someone who
was twice divorced [she said],
and who, according to prevailing standards –
Trump's [laughter] – was never more
than a Three, I suppose... It's silly to pretend
I never envied someone who could rouse
millions of people with one droopy eyelid.
But it's interesting: even at her sleekest, boldest,
most spandexed, it was always about
fertility. These supercouples aren't merely
fused, higher, Platonic
individuals – they have a greater range:
they do what we supposedly would,
if we could afford it. In her case bear,
adopt, and bear again, to make up for the world,
to be a kind of functioning UN.
(And of course they tend to
be liberals, for what would the other side
want with love, diversity, the Other?)
I watch with only the modicum
of envy I've confessed, because it gets
in the way: the point is to *be* them. And he –
so beautiful, so carefree, so
detached from whatever sincerity
the role demands, from even his other role,
the self... what else do straight people want
but to bring some man into focus, and he to escape?
I know whereof I speak
on this score, in a small way. We follow,
however abstractedly, rumours of dating
among the gods, for we want to see them try

like us to avoid
age, pills, the third drink,
the alien kids, the Agent who never calls
(there's always an agent, if not an author…)
Hopefully you won't grasp what I'm saying,
but drift as smoothly as you think and I pray
you will into that scene where someone's eyes
meet yours and there's no need to fantasize.

Ripped from the Headlines

One brother is a good earner
for the Mob, the other for a bank.
Mob brother lives in Brooklyn, other brother in Queens.
They meet periodically, under the radar,
preserving a sentiment so far uncostly.
Brooklyn's existence places
a lien on Queens that grows because
it isn't called in. Queens imagines
that if he were in some unimaginable
trouble, he could call on Brooklyn:
what's family for? Their conversations
over mid-level wine and pizza
are strong on sports and nostalgia (sports *are* nostalgia),
short on detail. Each maintains,
and feels in the other, that faith
(it's like a faith, far from analysis)
that merges ambition with what thwarts it.
Brooklyn's wife leaves him
for someone more sensitive. Queens's wife
finds a better earner.
Shortly thereafter, the bank throws
Queens under the bus for following orders:
assigning unsuspected credit cards.
Brooklyn, meanwhile, winds up for some reason
in landfill. It's like anything else –
when you can't play anymore, they tell you the rules.

Results May Vary

1

I was privileged to live
in immense luxury (it never seemed
that great to me) on the eve
of the Sixth Extinction-Level Event.
The Arctic ice-free in summer, Antarctica
thawing, most of the coral and 60% of vertebrates
dead since 1970 – but such phrases
sound like scolding,
and no one wants to be scolded. Yet
through subtle conduits, the anguish of frogs
and bears, the background noise
of energy in the atmosphere
seep into culture, and even I,
soigné as I am, have grown rude.
Observing my precipitous decay
with a *risus sardonicus* that is neither classical
nor Decadent nor brave nor
in any way generous, only
glad that I'll die before you, and in
some comfort. Like drowned bayous,
uncontainable
deserts and wildfires, methane belching from tundra,
my hate overflows its banks;
my 'narcissism of small differences'
(countless as the signs
at neofascist rallies
I watch on TV
with rage greater than theirs because informed)
flaps in the wind. And leaving places
I'll never visit and/or won't be invited to
again, I do once-unimaginably
vile things… 'Made you look!'

2

Orange lilies, pink alstroemeria,
one white rose and a ring
should do. Walking, I nervously
rearrange with my free hand
my straw hat, which alternates
with an upscale kerry and a bowler.
Then, ducking into door- and alleyways,
I change my look: thin eyebrows, small straight nose –
or the originals? Compress (there's a valve) gut and butt.
Lengthen legs and stride, then think
better of it. (Springs and struts.)
I wish there were a module for morale –
some slow-released hormone – and for the day:
Monet clouds, a brass band in the park, a park,
and a few last horse-drawn carts amidst
the Fords would be preferable
to this grey.
Will you say yes? Oh, do – before
I sense I've drifted back
into some Futurist future or Constructivist fancy,
and flights of biplanes mutate into drones,
and some medley of electronics,
first centralized and broadcast, then autonomous,
takes over regulating me.
Oh the Wellsian crowd is a Deco mirror
I wish we were gazing into
side by side, nude and organic;
but the gloom of the day and the world's prospects
have furnished only these flowers, as real as you.

3
The operative word is 'I' or 'buy';
they amount to the same thing.
With the decline of malls, malls are occupied
by artists, the lowest kind of squatter;
and these are the lowest kind of artist,
the audience – pretentious dreamers.
They drift through garbage, Everything Must Go
signs, needles, greasy wrappers.
They nap on the torn couches,
dream of Fifth Avenue, the secondhand smoke,
the contact high of money,
and gaze into the few working displays.
Dignity, a glazed bowl.
The give and take of discourse, a top.
The unarticulable early hope,
luggage(?). One place offers
(strange firms creep into dying malls)
a 'Love Machine.' The living dead,
readers, viewers, cognoscenti flock
to that window. They expect something
like an ancient fax or 3D printer,
concave, convex, and soulful; but what's there
is a man. He stares vulnerably out,
spreads his arms as if to embrace
the abandoned throng and the sullen vista
behind them. What the world
needs now, what the world
by definition needs is prosperity,
the carnal index of transcendent love;
moved by that vision, he begins to sing.

4

In her own much-loved work, the editor
moves from emotion A to emotion B.
It's apparently heroic for her to have
the first emotion, and the second,
and to move. I can't grasp those emotions.
Not much happens, but there's a lot of nature.
Someone or perhaps no one is there,
a betraying, reassuring presence.
For years before I learned the word 'reflux,'
I was troubled by heartburn.
Once walked at 3 AM to a 7/11
for Rolaids and the sort of high-carb crap
responsible for the condition. Once saw a diagram
of acid-producing cells in the stomach;
they looked like alien weapons or flowers.
When I chewed Tums or Rolaids or, in a pinch,
chugged milk, I visualized
the meeting between acid and chalky alkaline;
the brief cooling or neutrality
was blessed, though knowing that
the result is technically a 'soap'
caused qualms. This internal oil-war
changed some of my esophageal cells
to stomach cells. That's bad, said the doc
who stuck a tube down my throat,
then told me to take Prilosec daily.
Which stopped the problem for decades,
though recently I've heard it causes Alzheimer's.
When she encounters my work, the beloved editor
reacts first with a smile,
like any intellectual confronting terror.

Gnome Note

Fantasy would be forgivable
if it were understood
that Forest isn't easy. We require
space to recoup after deaths.
(The same holds true for deserts,
with their elder spirits.) Some of us
have a wider range than deer.
Others stay close to the cave but need
water. And we all breed circumspectly.
You'll never see us from a car.
Even horses, those opportunists
(their cynicism understandable),
ruin the neighbourhood. You can
only approach, if at all,
with supplies running out,
on your big ugly feet.

We the undersigned
reject your bigoted nonsense
that we represent a tribal, Oedipal,
or proto-hominid past. Such chutzpah!
We also demand
that you remove all steel and concrete
from our territory, and institute
a cull. It should be carried out
as humanely (so to speak) as possible:
we dislike loud noises.
You may shun the gaze of the selected
as long as you avoid ours.
Only when there are fewer
of you (amount to be determined)
shall we allow your gentle champion
to approach the princess, the gold.

The Companions

The first is ultimately responsible
for everything, but we don't blame him.
Dark matter, matter, dark energy, etc.
were not what he intended;
death was a total shock;
and all that was just one corner…
He has often tried to explain to us
his original idea
but needless to say it sounds impractical,
and in any case was instantly usurped
by something I can only visualize
as a scorpion. Now he's voluntarily old.
Since age for us entails
hesitation and apology,
he wears the wrinkles and the cane
as a way of apologizing.
And has lived since the onset
of time in a barred cottage,
chronicling the horrors to be repaid.

The second is swift and youthful,
less handsome than functional,
his smile the pilot light of his morale;
an obvious soldier.
He would, he says, reflect,
if there were something to reflect about.
There isn't; there is only the struggle,
where every cell and atom
and particle of folly is the front.
But those are my words, not his.
When we meet, he reports
curtly but thoroughly
on the latest depredation,
and the old man writes in his black notebook.

Then we eat. No living things are harmed
in the preparation of these meals,
though none of us is vegetarian,
and drink a harsh Rioja or Mourvèdre,
recalling blood. Then –
cigar, cigarettes, and pipe – we bring out
the heavy cards (my role is to cut and deal),
which as they fall
avenge, heal, annul.

'And Hearts that We Broke Long Ago'

The door closes; the one
who understood you a moment
recedes on whichever side.
You're amazed you retained so much
sentimentality – that you cherished,
unknowing, a category
like 'being understood.'
And wonder if you could recapture
that warmth.
But since the door closed, time has elapsed.
Pick a date between now and
the heat-death of the universe:
that much time has already passed,
the distance between you that much greater.

The halls are clean, wood polished, light complex.
Perhaps destruction itself
will save from destruction these places
where most of your errands and duties
still lie.
Though secretly you prefer the waste grounds
free of investment
with their occasional grunts of grief and terror,
not one addressed to you, you uttering none.
Birds peck at their mites and invisible things
rising from asphalt after rain.
Birds fill, in a manner of speaking,
the space between earth and sky,
and you are not responsible for them.

Recognition

The figure in the mirror is always a clown.
But it has been decided
by that cultic power-behind-the-throne
which is called the middle class that clowns
are frightening to children, and therefore frightening.
Committees of clowns
protest this unfair meme, with no more success
than other efforts of organized labour.
Now, with the clowns in exile, jail,
or shantytowns that once were circuses,
who will entertain children
at birthday parties, weddings,
and trendy celebrations of divorce?
Kids cry for their old trauma.
It looks like the job will be left
to amateurs. In the mirror,
I try to gauge objectively my skill
and appeal. Balloon animals squeak
painfully as I construct them; one
pops. A card, it is actually not
the right card, drops from my hand, then the whole deck.
I can already hear
them crying at my gig – from ambivalence,
frustration? Perhaps the new horror
is not being dressed as a clown, only a grownup.

Let Us Hear from You

To find one's genetic material
swirled with that of siblings brings
a glow, a sense of having passed
directly from before- to afterlife.
Especially when milk,
benign and impersonal, the substance of grace
itself, enters, and brief stinging showers
of pepper and paprika, and particles of herb
like wreaths. But all this joy
sinks suddenly into an acid bath –
butter and mushrooms, beside, *within* one,
they too giving up
their moisture, their nature. Crusted
the colour of earth, one suffers a moment
of knowledge: I could have been a contender,
a hen or rooster. And of
hatred: May this fact stick in their craws
like a piece of our shells, may it clog their disposal!
I mean those who loom like evil worlds
and stab and cut and salt and call us good.

The Upper Terrace

I feel genuinely sorry
for scientists who come to me
to complain that despite the satellites,
quantum computers, containment labs,
and particle accelerators I've
provided absolutely free,
they can't find anything –

no atom, no particle;
cells, but without those busy vulnerable
parts; even light
seems what it was for Goethe –
no spectrum, just white.
They have nothing to do, to learn.
They project the innocence

of math types and math; some
like music, but for relaxation's sake;
and all are as deferential
as if I were a funder. Beyond the terrace,
an apparently G-type sun
presides over diamond mountains
and similarly whimsical

rivers and seas. Great birds honk.
I tell them they could switch – it shouldn't
require much retraining – to
psychology (mine)
and formulate models
based on genetics and influences
from childhood; I'll give them all the data

I have. Or (I refill glasses) they
could try art theory. But
they look so wounded I feel guilty,
and promise to recreate in their labs
the universe they know. Let them have at it,
and if they're very good
I'll tell them how it ended.

Boxed Set

In all the years I used
the university library
(fifty books per semester), only once
did someone else want
a book I had out.
Which gives you some idea.
It gave *me* some idea,
and might have proved instructive
to the ever-ambivalent ingenus
of Bucharest and Lisbon,
to the woman self-pursued
across London, to the assayers
of nothingness, which has different weights
and smells, to the partisans of leaves
and snow, to half-apologetic
or not-at-all apologetic
fascists, to Europe generating always more
Europe, more disproofs
of capital, more capital,
to the woman who gazed
at the no longer bleeding
bodies of her family
splayed over a century, to
those who saw truths
smaller than superstrings –
all these and more would hear
in the record of my checkouts,
Oh brothers, swine, comrades, nobody wants us.

The Print

Almost lost on a wall
between an unkempt bookcase and a place
where plaster had fallen, a framed,
glassed, sepia blur.
I had to set my tea, long cold,
precariously on a patch of shelf
before I could visually edit
dust from the glass, and the reflection
of the distant lamp, and slowly
something, someone beautiful emerged.
'I've had that a long time,'
the old man said. 'I'm not sure of the provenance.
You'd like to think an extraordinarily
talented young fellow sketched her,
all that love and desire
at odds with draftsmanship until
he reconciled them in the final print.
And then 'went off' or 'was called up'
to war somewhere and died,
and *she* is all that's left. You don't
assume – notice – a self-portrait.
If you do, what happens to the story?
There's no young man; she's coolly aware of
or wistful in advance for her own beauty.
Or he exists, and she sends it
to his bivouac, trench, or airfield,
and either he brings it home or it's returned.
Or just conceivably she makes it after
receiving the telegram, as a sort
of message to him in the other world,
a memento of his gaze, his love, his care.
I like to think that love escapes
not only death but ambiguity
and does some nameless unexpected work.
Much as the motivations, vain and cruel,

behind an ancient pile give way
to an insight, fleeting and cliché
as may be, in the tourist who explores it.
Or the way life presents
to the child it drags along
a precis of himself, which he or she
eventually, detachedly admits;
although discounted, rounded-off material
may still return as visions and regrets.'

Sobornost

It's one of those songs on the edge
of Easy Listening, pushed over
by whoever devises music
for malls, chain restaurants, and hair salons.
It gets me. Suddenly the pathos
of a man who tells a woman (the
singer) of all his betrayals
by other girls, realizing
at last that she's the one for him,
is *my* pathos, though actually
I never experienced it.
I miss not having experienced it.
As I listen I experience it
in some sense, and my eyes grow moist.
But actually, at that moment,
there's more: saving money, buying a house,
staying clean, having kids, likeable bosses
are possible, the yard, the car
more than the sum of their parts, the lawn
one among others, all neighbours friends,
shoulder to shoulder, life, fulfillment
possible – all this in
that song which gets me, the equivalent
(without all the soulfulness) of what Russians
call 'us-ness.'

Tulum

From the terrace of the Temple
of the Descending God, the High Priest
addresses the crowd. He wears white,
they dirtier white. Since birth his skull has been shaped –
bone is soul – into a quasi-godlike lozenge.
He holds a cordless mic, has no idea
what it is, how he's saying what he's saying,
or why he understands it. The crowd – they live
in thatched huts that will soon return to jungle –
assimilate the moment to the divine
because everything is part of the divine,
though soon this basic ontological
assumption feels threatened, which results

in tension. Ages past, says the priest,
a big rock fell into the sea
from the cold that lies beyond the sky. What was sea-floor
became the flat land. No lakes or rivers formed,
and very little topsoil. What rain there was
seeped through the limestone. Matters weren't helped
by felling trees to burn wood to make lime
for temples. That's why you're poor, he adds,
and touches his weird head. Abruptly,
the remaining trees are largely replaced
by lawn, the lower castes by tourists;
the effect, he thinks, or something like him thinks,
is more Watteau than Claude; and then

it's gone. So is the microphone.
His gestures, praying for rain and health
and captives, are big ideograms;
the people's, more restrained but equally legible.
Still, for a moment, passing overhead,
a ragged local crow is just a bird;
the gods are what they are beneath their paint;
the self too, fractured, friable – in fact
there *is* a self; it has no function. Vaguely,
the priest resolves to think about all this
(but what?) when the rites are done and he
returns to the stone House of the High Priest,
where he lives in a cool darkness, between columns.

Tough Crowd

A comedian towards the end of a failed gig
cries 'I'm dying, here,' then really *looks*
at the Play-Doh faces in the semi-dark
and thinks, That may in fact be true,
or true for me, inadequate for them;
and in the silence, unbroken even
by cellphones, glassware, farts or jeering,
goes on, because what else is there to do,
tries new and no material, amuses
himself, confesses, mourns, considers
how Lenny Bruce before the end
was called 'the rabbi,' no longer seeking
laughs or trying to be at all endearing.

Bear with Flag

Reports disputed whether it
was white or bore a symbol – something
oval, a pinecone, a pawprint,
a salmon – and if so, that was even more
remarkable, said scientists
(who are always trying to get us
to marvel); but in any case
the flag got lost. There was also, apparently,
a battered, slowly leaking
beach ball he was balancing on
when spotted; that too was misplaced.
Then only his talking was left,
which many people denied despite
the tapes (though not the older local
Inuits in the parking lot
who insisted they understood).
Opinion was he was *trained*,
a hoax – perhaps on the part of
the scientist who thrust a mic
at his muzzle and asked how an asocial
species had found a spokesman; the bear
was heard to say, 'Come any closer
I'll bite your arms off.' He may
have hurt his case by not mentioning
a mate and cubs that (film indicated)
had drowned; and by repeatedly
and pretty clearly claiming he was the last,
though there were ten. Reporters
decided he was simply nuts – no doubt
traumatized; when someone
mentioned 'extinction' he seemed to smile and
growl happily, 'That's a big word… a *big* word.'

Kin

By the late seventeenth century he is
at least possible, crying 'Bring out
your dead' and breaking into
houses where the distinction
is moot; where the doctors
with great beaked masks full of posies
have been and gone or never came; where
the floor is rife with ichor and the air
with odors he no longer notices,
except the sweet distinctive one
of plague; where he orders
his boys to hoist and bind
to the overladen cart the once-
fat shitbag, the rag-doll girl,
the mother slumped in the last poor soup
(which luckily doused
the fire) – 'Mind you don't slip
in the slop,' he says, and they laugh,
like machines; all pockets theirs,
all purses his, all silver and gold
the king's, but the king won't miss
this single taper; he's also
welcome, His Majesty is, to
that crucifix and to believing
there's a point to all this.

The Sect

1

It was one of ours who approached Kerouac,
deliberately too late, just before the end –
the great man alarmed, disgusted
by kids, admirers, talking what they thought was
his style; and they were dirty, sinful,
in no way recognizably Catholic
or anything. Our agent, planning subtly to mention
ojos, mandalas, drugged fireworks
in Mexico City before it became
hell, meanwhile asked some
detail about other geniuses,
met when and where. And the writer,
his liver almost fully defeated,
said, 'It doesn't matter
where I went or who I saw or what
I did.' Which, our spy wrote, showed
'a man getting ready to leave this world,'
but that was a coded circumlocution –
he knew and we know
it's never the whole story –

2

The time machine is self-effacing,
masked as a horse-trough, horse-dung,
or an especially stolid horse –
all numerous in this dusty German town,
which to our man looks dead to the point of undeath,
but to Marx seems hurtling towards
justice. It's 1848.
He agreed to a half-hour's talk.
Though it has stretched to three hours
on the bench beside the trickling fountain (which
like every amenity bears
a plaque thanking some duke or other),

he, young, short-bearded, hulking, has not lost
that lowering mien, disdainful
of fools, that made his *Junghegelianer*
friends call him 'Moor'. Our adept has laid out
the miscalculations and surprises;
quoted Bernstein, Bebel, Bernays, Gramsci,
Ford, Trotsky in '05 and '40,
Zuckerberg, Deng Xiaoping;
enumerated martyred workers, their efforts
inadequate; suggested adding
two new terms to the yet-unwritten
formula $M - C - M_1$.
We chose him for his voice,
as soft and irrefutable
as rain. Marx listens, asks two or three questions,
abruptly stands and strides away.
Our chap presumably does not attempt
to follow; we don't know. He fingers
the gold coins in his pocket,
stares off at dust, bad water, toothache, exile.
The world just born will be perhaps a better one,
but won't in any case be his world, ours,
which, farther and farther away, goes on as before.

3

Our holy rites are not limited
to preserving for decades the rooms of lost children,
as if one morning they
will reconstruct themselves from the DNA
in pillows and step forth, as Lazarus should have…
For many of us it's we
ourselves who live in such a room,
though it only exists in the discomfort
we feel in other rooms;
or never quite exists,
which makes it more secure. And often the space
is further reduced, to, say,
an unforgotten doll

at the back of the cupboard of a man of affairs
and/or his strange remissness in affairs. It isn't
only evil stalkers
who make walls into shrines,
with photos, stolen garbage, expressionist
drawings; many would flee
if they met their cynosures,
if the latter existed, which often they don't.
There are so many gods.
We generate them, they fill all empty layers.
Candles play a role –
not as mindless atmospherics,
nor as a symbol, but as critique,
a clamorous demand on the rest of space.
In dimness and quiet,
often hard to achieve, reverent fingers
approach a yellowed page, an ancient Playmate
(gaze eerily intimate), things on a desk
or in a cupboard; and
the formula one speaks is one
one knows one has invented.

4

One drab spiritual exercise
(it has, like the rest, no aim beyond itself)
is to tell a brother how he sees you,
then listen as he tells how you see him.
An aging black man says
I'm listening for traces of accent,
patois, or the shoulder-chip bestowed
by escape from the pincers of
his childhood and crude whites; am wondering
how spontaneous and happy
the professional suit and diction are, and which
profession they suggest. And I say
he sees an old Jew,
i.e., a facial sub-expression shared
by tailor, poet, swindler, judge –

the trace of some long-past divorce
from God on grounds of non-consummation.
He objects that I'm evading self
in tribe. I mull and discard
various quips. The clatter of the Automat,
old busboys slinging trays like guilt,
the clang of fedoras on metal hatstands,
alternates with the homogenized
hush of an internet café. For the sect
is equally not at home
in any era, and tends to drift
in search of comfort… Outside,
crowds cheer a famous victory and kiss,
then scream and flee from drones. We may not even
know each other, sharing a table
only because crowding abrogated
the law (one soul, one table).
We may not even speak,
observing thus the basic
methodology of the sect. Yet each of us knows
that at any moment punks
in ski-masks may barge in and shoot
the ceiling. Or a noisy squad
of soldiers seeking good rough fun,
or enemies in general, or us.

5

Reassurances from her parents
are insufficiently articulate
and impassioned. She perceives the lie:
it isn't baby fat
but structural, a bulbous Saxon chin,
short neck, small eyes, critiqued with more precision
than beauty expends on itself. So she withdraws
from mirrors, and at ten,
in a softer, more effective form
of cutting, refuses Facebook.
Her cellphone has one number: home.

She has already perfected
the rare knack of invisibility
at school. Evades, when they come,
the incubi of boy-bands, boy-stars,
dreams. Her otherworld –
she reflects that this may be what lonely boys,
if there are any, want – is a *group*,
with her the sardonic, greying, indispensable
chief. She bends her scholarship
to find them, half-prepared to learn
they too are just an otherworld. That's how we recruit.

6

One *can* return, however, from the future.
R&R some forty million
years hence; long dull ride.
We have a sort of campground there,
rudimentary. Volleyball.
The animals who inherit
(they look a bit like mice and otters,
are all thumbs) insist they're animals,
and not intelligent, though they plainly are.
They tolerate us, but man is neither
a myth to them nor an object of study;
they like to stroll deacidified shores
and sail refurbished coral reefs.
That's as far as they get. The stars seem
a little farther. Our hosts
enjoy sunsets enormously, at great, silent,
contemplative length. And they build pebble paths
through deserts to shrines
they can't or see no need to
explain – we understand such things.
Whales are gone, sharks walk. The sea
will last a while but seems not especially vital;
the new trees etiolated, pseudo-savage.
But time and the metaphysics
of time occasion much discussion,

which we're invited to share as long as we can.
Death, black holes, the fate of galaxies
show up as minor metaphors. Our friends view
themselves as lovers, serfs, curators of time.

7

As such they communicate
with a rock star of the classic era,
the sort who destroyed guitars, hotel rooms, virgins,
and was widely loved.
He sees them first as new hallucinations,
their messages as weird dyslexic riffs.
But the effect their words have
is perhaps unintended: he announces
(first to a groupie, then the press) that rock
is the music of time, it serves time;
its rhythm is that of machines; if it's sex
it's machine sex, and he won't be its slave
any more. He is even less coherent
than usual, and reporters
play him for comedy henceforth.
He's rich but not enough to afford
the isolated house,
the tutoring, the unstoned months
meditating on the last movement
of Vaughn Williams' Fourth, the lost-in-space
adagio of Tippett's Third, the brooding arcadias
of Babbitt and Feldman. He discovers
that life without an entourage
or drugs is hard, has no mystical-transcendent
advantage. When he isn't studying,
he stares at a wall. It doesn't change.
That may be what they wanted
to tell me, he thinks. The dark sun Where Are They Now
has risen and he's broke and can't
get anyone to perform
the piece he ultimately writes, the music of nothing.

8

Meanwhile the world, without leaving its couch,
runs, leaps, as swift as doomed gazelles,
towards the only happiness:
the kind that need not doubt itself
or ever encounter doubt,
that may destroy all designated threats
and is destruction... Who would not envy
minds for whom the speed of change,
scary, becomes denatured and benign
in the pure speed of images?
Life, the punch press, meaning will return,
the alien, the ambiguous will be made
to leave, and one need not be polite to them.
We recognize much in this new world:
life *is* a dream.
Unfortunately, worlds don't realize
that dreams are private, repay analysis,
and must be hidden by a wall…
Eventually they'll come for us,
not as ourselves but as some other evil
minority. Each man takes his own evil
with him to death; we'll take ours to the camps
or the wall. While above our ashes, leaders
whose charmlessness is their charisma promise
what can be promised: blood,
and what can't: love for the loveless.

9

But occasionally a brother or sister
snaps. Wants light, to shed light;
to reverse the internal figure
and ground; to impart *leçons des ténèbres*.
Sets up a crate (few really
contained soap) in a park or on a corner.
But this unfortunately always happens *now*,
when everyone relies on social media.
It's just a disturbance. Cops

appear swiftly, and
one's message is compressed into a tweet.
And even lifelong members of the sect
waste time justifying, explaining
the self, alluding to, footnoting
(weepily) the past; the old meme of *witness*
breaks against the prevailing
contempt for anything that sticks out.
So the rhetor desperately turns
to abstraction, moralism, verse,
which soon devolve into a rage
greater than the apathy
of the nonexistent crowd, or
vice versa. It doesn't matter
whether, from handcuffs, you cry *There are other worlds*
or *Aliens want to help*
but you're all so damned passive – which
is fine; you'll need more help… or lose
all interest, idly gauging the proportion
in the crowd of tinfoil hats to religious headgear.

10

If you survive the night and are bailed out,
you go home. Day looks wrong on the wall;
you wait for evening.
Perhaps you pride yourself on having no
more things than would be available
in a just austerity. But the point
of twilight is to weaken your connection
even to those and the wish for justice.
Also the thought-stoppingly
obvious thought occurs that home
belongs to a bank or landlord; you have here
no continuing city.
Which fact, especially at twilight,
can be a cause of peace – you're a guest,
guests check out; but that's just twilight talking,
and that shameless collaborator sleep.

Better to bank, to concentrate
the wealth of being left alone
a moment. Lovers, friends
from the past appear, not as memories
but as universes budded off
from yours. They progressed, they were happy,
no one died.
Likewise ideas return, confident and solid
elsewhere. Amidst the never-distant sounds
of sirens, televisions, quarrels, your labouring
fridge and heart, as sundered and determinate
as stars, they wait for you to complete your training.

Opus Posthumous

The devil tells you the truth about yourself.
You might think God does that,
in a nicer way. But really, what
gentility could make up for being told…
Well, you know what he'll say.

I've long since reconciled myself to being
only remembered subatomically,
my work a potentially retrievable
algorithm, a merely structural
element, like cement. But lately

I had a vision: future readers reading
and weeping over my crass,
sardonic oeuvre, even resurrecting
print and paper for its sake, seeing only
sighs and love and fleeting beauty.

Touch

Perhaps after forty bad years I would have
answered direct questions
about my life, my case,
without drama or affect but also
without excessive affectlessness;
without even my favorite piece
of chinoiserie: *Alas,*
Fortune did not smile on me
in this world, because in that world
I would, so to speak, have chosen
ingenuousness over show.
And the one who had questioned me
would be saddened, moved, would ask
if there was something she could do,
and I, objective as always, would say No;
enshrining, no doubt,
the moment in my heart. Or not.

Nostalgia

My taste for ruins and waste places
extends to philosophy. In the mental south,
the fatuously mirrored and fractal towers
of poststructuralism rise. I haunt
instead the abandoned mill towns of
the north. (You'll notice
decaying allegorical tropes.) Here things are things,
frayed narratives
still snap over empty schools, time although questionable
provides the only light,
and language doesn't matter but poetry might.

Here too my hand moves down a thigh
and across and beneath a breast,
the same way these things and the moon
and the lamp on a bureau shine:
forever. Because time is not
disposal but storage. We
were always there and always are. What's needed
is focus, which creates eternity.
While on a shelf nearby
is her subjective reaction, part of 'the mind'
the moment she was pleased with me.

Flight

The architect had tried to elaborate
'stairs,' but what is there
besides grandeur and discouragement
for the frail and short of breath?
Carved idle banisters, sea-monsters no doubt
representing what authority views as free.
The buildings pierced by the steps
like mountains by a mountain road
may have housed priests, accountants, whores,
but mainly tried to look classical.

The workers gathered at the foot,
between the sea-monsters' fangs.
The soldiers at the top
fixed bayonets. It was sometime between steam
and cellphones, and the distant
phone-booth I stood in
was a white faux-marble pagoda.
But the receiver dangled silent,
so that was modern, and the graffiti,
though neatly written, were apolitical
and foul. I held the receiver
to my ear, to look innocent if the fleeing
crowd and its pursuers came this far;
the image was of parting a stampeding
herd, and I felt

ashamed. The workers,
unarmed except for songs and banners, started
up. The soldiers, already firing,
descended in good order.
Officers shot into heads. In an hour, a morgue-wagon
came for bodies
no one had collected; these had been left on the steps.
Which other workers soon came to hose down.

The Shadow Knows

He decided early that his parents
were the wrong ones. There had been some plot
or mistake. Learning later
by obscure means that this is a common
illusion, he thought All those people can't
be wrong; then that the implication You're
nuts was also part of the masquerade.

In later life, experiences of
exclusion on the pretext that he smelled bad
suggested a wider error, and he
was forced to juggle various
responses: I hate them.
I forgive them. There's just too
many of them. They know not what they do.

Gudrun

A superheroine – hit by a ray
from some opponent, or victim
of a rip in the entire comics universe –
found herself in an Edwardian novel.
Briefly glimpsed, she was attributed
to overwork; then her cloaking device
gave her time to suss out the situation.
Petticoats, corsets, the mincing walk,
the inconsistent ironclad repressions,
the horse shit – not for a moment
would she adjust to this;
her options were to revolutionize it,
somehow return to her world,
or both. But the compound sentences
swirling around black holes
of insinuation, the ten-course meals
of ambivalence, the body-
and eyebrow-language gauged
in microns, the stupidity like fat
in proletarian roles
hampered her: it was like moving,
talking, through glue. Men gazed
at her legs and armored bustier and,
bereft of coherent speech,
grabbed. Cops grabbed. They
had to be dealt with. Eventually,
unable to communicate
with monumentally male
scientists, she appropriated
a manor house, achieved
a standoff with the army
and press, performed in a tower
what experiments she could.
Despair, she found, is depth, an endless
echo in a dark and vaulted room.

But she wouldn't let it get to her. Kept up
her powers – local ploughboys
took off their caps before their clothes –
and looks: a ten-K run each morning.
Plates rattled, as she passed, in cabinets,
and stained-glass windows in the roadside church.

Running Lights

The romantic illusion of
the immediate… but who wouldn't want that
here, with waves only high enough
to shiver moonlight, the mansions
on the distant cape reduced
to bigger, yellower stars? Perhaps the great,
white, silent, circling bird – 'That's no gull!' –
was also hired by the caterer.
If it comes round again I'll say,
'It's an albatross. It's blessing us
because we let it live,' thus turning
some arc of conversation towards my interests.
If talk resumes… it may not. The tuxes
are deeper, gowns more vivid bits of dark;
the waiters in their whites, atoning gulls.
The breeze, combining brine, perfume, hors-d'oeuvres
works; the drinks are gold, the candles dim.
It could be night has gotten through to them –
boastfulness, even if unjustified,
sated, competitiveness
tranced, the various
hyper- and dystrophies of soul and market
position zeroed out… And I
can almost feel, almost pretend
I belong, no more a shadow than these shadows,
my evening wear no less skin-deep
than theirs, my importance nil, my profession
weird of course but acceptable, since I was,
mysteriously, invited… It's
the port side, yes, the port side
I'm looking over, out to sea. One should
be able to merge with the in(de)finite
from anywhere, even a yacht. One should
by my age be more… be less…
But now our host appears, from the lower decks.

Life-giving gossip, selective information
revive; moon, sea, and stars disappear
though I, alone, keep looking for them. He
eventually looms beside me, saying,
'A friend of mine, a psychologist,
took an interest in a murderer. Fifteen. Guilty.
After many sessions, the kid said
what he really wanted was to sit by a river, fishing.
My friend, though glad to have gained his trust,
still felt the little punk was missing something.'

Note to Cavafy

The barbarians are no kind of solution
to the acedia of the city. They want to loot, rape, kill,
and more than likely they get off
on torture. Their gods,
big sexy people who can fly, turn to fire,
turn enemies to ice, shoot webs from their palms,
are mere spectacle. Only the subtlest
philosopher would seek archetypes in them;
all he could learn is that there are no archetypes.
If the barbarians stay, their initial
rubble will be cleared or interest tourists
while the half-breed masters of the future
revive an ancient angst.

Actually, city itself is an unwarranted
assumption. The basic state, now reemerging
everywhere, has two parts: a) barbarians; b)
some old fart, offed when he gets sick enough,
who meanwhile owns the pigs, potato fields,
all the remaining guns, the women,
the big wall and its guards. The nomad
chieftains also kill their chief;
the old man understands this, feels a bond
that never leads to truce. They want what he has;
they understand each other. The essential
war involves no cultural differences,
inspires no poems and doesn't end.

Crag

Gradually you no longer signal.
Nothing less than an aircraft carrier
would do, and the only one that appears
is that laughable Russian one,
their only one, which Putin deployed to Syria –
how did it get here?
Yet even if the whole Sixth Fleet
and a Chinese missile cruiser
sailed by, you wouldn't wave. The giant
subs of the corporations are more enticing,
but they don't show themselves.

Each morning the sun claps
its helmet on you, corrects and molds its pupil.
Your companions now are heroes, ancient broadcasts:
Rios Montt, who assured Guatemalans
that their skin was as blue as their flag, the fallen
visionary Nixon, stern father Duterte, Trump the evangel.
Love is the dark companion of the sun.
Sex is the fantasy that (quite gently,
given the circumstances) usurped memory.
You have learned and will learn. Like a saint,
you will eat and drink only learning.
Among the rocks, ranks of stones
that your blood has blessed are your soldiers.
Your last regret is that no rags remain
to give them flags; you have resolved upon
their emblem:
the Iguana beats the Eagle, Bear, and Dragon!

Two Views of Escape

1

Even so close to it, drones, patrols,
sweaty prayers for one's fake ID,
nights in sewers, dead factories and the attics
of heroes ready to give up can make one
give up. Early on, we lost an old man.
He had pills, promised to use them.
Would have liked to say, 'You go, I'll hold them off,'
or something of the sort, but wasn't armed.
Now this guy, not so old,
starved like the rest but still walking, says,
'I can't.' One flashlight glance shows
he's lost it; we'll lose him anyway.
And like all those who can't adjust,
he makes a speech. 'We're ruled by
a cartoon. *I'm* a cartoon.
I'm old enough to remember: under
Reagan, people who had always been
antiwar, pro-civil-rights etc. suddenly
gave up all that, cared only for
their portfolios, real estate, maybe cars and yoga.
The phrase was, they were 'blooming.'
I'm going to wait for the police,
and when they come I'll jump out, yell
'Hi, guys!', big gesture, and maybe I too
will regain the third dimension. Bloom.'

2

We emerge from stinking tunnels into
cityscape that can't cram enough
grandeur or too many types of grandeur
into itself. Domes, ruins;
glass towers unlike those we knew:
inviting, truly transparent. Day cool
but incandescent. Birds – the vivid ones:
jays, redwings. Parks winding towards
a castle, long the people's. The people avoid
our smell but it doesn't deter them:
they would take us individually home,
give us wine and baths and wholesome soup and wait
for our tears. But our rescuers,
though in no way constraining us,
discourage this. And we too
think it better to lower
our gaze, limp silently through
a city kind to all the senses, every
yearning. The fresh-painted huts,
well-built and -insulated, didn't
require a chain-link fence but we prefer it.
It's good to be clean, warm, fed,
stare secretively out or watch TV,
take our meds, talk twice weekly
with therapists about freedom.

Beatus

An angel is like a doctor or lawyer.
It says when you've done something stupid, and
advises you to keep your mouth shut – like,
don't eat. The neuter pronoun
merely observes the old convention of
androgyny; what counts is the tone,
which you could hear from either gender if
you listened. Sometimes, inappropriately,
you weep, ask for a hug,
suggest that you expected more…
extensive counsel. The angel
looks blank, then professorial.
Traditionally, it says, we had two roles,
vengeance and comfort. But in modern times,
questions arose: What
exactly is being avenged, who comforted?

Aglaea

I'm on my way to her
on roads that never felt the tramp of Rome,
which makes her name somewhat anomalous, but
so what. I imagine her baking,
long braids pinned back, cheeks red, arms floury.
There's laughter, talk, a pump, an open fire,
she and the ambience absurdly lovely.
Which doesn't mean I *expect* her to bake,
or find in my approach exclusive joy,
or not sculpt or not do theoretical physics (if
she wished and the environment allowed);
she just likes baking. The local
tech may be passé but my views are modern.

The sun seems near, noon prolonged.
No robbers haunt the woods, or ghosts the crossroads.
In the villages a wayfarer can rely
on water, straw, an apple; but
a meal, a shower of sorts, and bed require
muscle (though no special competence).
The barn goes up, the harvest in.
The men are unopinionated.
Bells mark six-hour intervals, nothing more,
are rung by a sophisticated clockwork,
and the buildings that support them, weathered stone
outside, inside are white abstraction;
perhaps an inner chamber of decision.

The above is a composite
of places ever nearer to my sweetheart
(there are cities but they scarcely matter).
Mothers are charmed but see no point
to my songs about space flight and bras.
Their girls, however... In one village,
throughout a winter then the spring, I linger
and learn what tale I have to tell:
Even where armies, churches, rage,
the patriarch and king are gone, as in
a strange joint dream of Blake and Jefferson,
betrayal remains, and guilt, the lazy
drift of self in self. Aglaea, farewell.

N.J.

I imagine that the dot-com boom
brought microbreweries, boutiques,
and a few condos to the downtown. Now
they're empty too, and, though distorted,
the profile of the place conforms to memory.
And the house they let him go to die in
after the electroshocks failed, or worked,
may have fresh paint on all its gables
(the money that shows up where there is none!)
or be gone. By all accounts
(one) he was as crack-voiced and foul-learnèd
as ever at the end,
just slower. If I knew where his grave was
I might visit it, if I visited
that town. He would appear in flat daylight
and ask what brought me here
after fifty years, and understand when I said
nothing in particular.

Why the Classics

I'm revived. Still don't know where or when,
but why, I think, is up to me.
(At least that has a calm heroic ring.)
When I wake, my collected unpublished works,
well-xeroxed, spiral-bound, clear plastic covers,
lie around me in boxes. Shit, I think,
they can't manage at least a flash-drive? –
but later I see, if not the point, a symbol.
And the room is nice and, once I decode the instructions,
can be stuffed, life's-work and all, into
a pocket of my cargo shorts.
The honcho races in this galaxy
resemble a weepy giant tardigrade
and a cross between a squid and an old typewriter.
I travel, seeking a publisher.
But the tardigrades only perceive the Ideal,
and the remingtons are great bullshitters. Something
I can't describe kicks me out of its office
when I try to explain Confessional poetry.
At last a gentle machine species
says it will take a look. But the problem,
as always, is accessibility.
What's a father? What's capitalism?
Why is the speaker of this poem
so unhappy? Few sentients will understand
his mating habits. Instead of mourning
the past, why doesn't he go there
and change it? If we publish this, the text
will be almost entirely footnotes;
and readings – even if we could provide
the right atmosphere – might be awkward.
They leave me sitting with my boxes.
I can take as long as I want… (I've run
into humans, sort of, here and there,
but they've little to say for themselves.)

Non Omnis

As they walk with my coffin,
the pallbearers notice
it's heavier. Though their expressions
remain somber, each thinks, He was a
big guy, but what's in there?
Secret journals, first editions?
A bowling ball?
Cords almost break as I'm lowered –
consternation, grotesqueness! But then
I'm quiet. Custodians will tell you, every
graveyard is full of creaking, shiftings,
gas. But from me not a peep.
What's happening is subatomic:
a densification, a gathering
of bosons, as yet unsuspected
by physics. Insofar as I can, I promise
I won't sink to the centre of the earth,
provoking vulcanism, disturbing others.
There's merely a rock, oddly shaped,
metamorphic beyond granite, beyond diamond.
The seas rise, fall, sea floors
become new continents, have little or no
effect on my point of view;
perhaps a vaguely elegiac tone,
at times inappropriate... Sun reaches out.
Earth otherwise gone,
I form new orbits. Black holes
eventually taste and expel me,
until with the last particles but mine,
they too decay. My body drifts alone
till I need it again.

B-movie

The hard drawl suits
her wheat-stalk beauty,
remarkably uneclipsed
by a bruise and black eye. Arms
crossed amid the hazmat-suited Feds
in the lab beneath her slovenly
kitchen, all 'God Bless This House,' she's like
'I don't know nothin'.' The black agent
(whom she of course hates
and who is clearly marked for doom) talks
softly about bruises
while the star,

scowling, in latex gloves, examines
the lab. In a flashback, the villain
draws blood, exhales into
a tube, inspires himself by gazing
at the Nazi regalia
on a wall of the lab. The girl
is crying, now. 'He was mean,'
she confides to the black agent.
We see the villain driving,
an innocuous metal cylinder
on the seat beside him. 'He concentrated
his whole personality, his
essence,' says the star

or another (probably less doomed)
sidekick, a scientist.
'He's going to release it into the atmosphere!'

North Shore

Mills long since closed, but these are suburbs,
not towns, and the looming
wealthy city keeps,
more or less, the ball rolling:
after five years, the crack
is replastered, the fallen
brick removed; after ten, wormy boards
are replaced (it's all bricks here, and wood
beneath some neon)
while halfway down an obscure though largely
treeless side street a house
is repainted, purple, green, or cheerful orange.
The avenue bends but never curves.
Its name is changed but seldom shown.
The streetlamps of this district lack
those heartening vaguely-feudal hanging banners.
Pizza serves Bail Bonds, Tavern both;
Nails lives in hope, One-Day Blinds
and Toys in greater. The parkas of
pedestrians need not be as dark
as the day. However slow the traffic,
it's faster than the fellow with
two canes, who to the side-mirror grants
his look.

Strange to Think

Strange to think that in ancient times
I lived quite happily
like a slob (though I mainly,
ungallantly and truthfully blame
the girl I lived with). Surveying our piles
I often cried, 'In ancient times
a pig ran through here,' to which she added,
'Saying wee wee wee wee!!' Which,
with my portentous mythic tone,
was the signal; and friends
(the friends of that time, of youth,
specifically of youth that had no contacts
or capital) mysteriously gathered.
Some lived, more windowlessly
than we, downstairs, some in nearby crates.
Soon I had changed into my bright
green shorts and flip-flops, wrestled
the vacuum cleaner from a closet, removed
my shirt, put on the necklace
of hanging plastic skulls. To our already
stoned and Frito-spreading friends, I
explicated the vacuum cleaner: 'Him
Big Suck! Him have no mercy!!'
There's a film somewhere, in landfill. When
Lebowski was there, always lucid,
expounding the first platform of
the Students for a Democratic Society, I
ascribed a class analysis
to Big Suck. Then I turned it on, poking
the piles (which my girlfriend, theoretically,
was removing, redistributing), prodding
her feet and those of our friends. The
apartment offered some resistance, but
it would be cleaned.

Bad Hair Day

I wouldn't know. I can imagine
hour after hopeless hour
of faux pas, excessive or insufficient
tact, lost files, the assholedom
of bosses, and that's just work-life, followed
over drinks by temblors
in already unstable friendships,
malign attempted pickups,
heartburn, punctuated throughout
by failed rebrushing. Inexplicable
curse, its own stigmata,
gone on the morrow with everything
again lovely enough… As I say,
I wouldn't know. Men in these matters
as in so many are unjustly free,
and anyway Mother left me the gift
of baldness. Which is like
a coat of ever-fresh police-station
green on the concrete wall
of sanity. Ephemera, disgust for one's
inert or defeated self are
burnt off, with hair, from within. It is,
as Marinetti said, 'a sign of genius!!
Proof: myself. Mussolini.'

Romance of the Form

It's one of those bureaucratic things
you can't do online; to avoid lines,
go early. There you find the wait is short,
the lighting less than awful,
and soon you're presenting your documents.
A poster: Kafka's face
(the opposite of a hypnotist,
he knew you'd never look into his eyes),
circled in red with a red diagonal,
over pledges of transparency and service.
The girl across the counter (nametag ATHENA)
is to die for,
but her dark and classic features
suggest melancholy. Which –
as you turn the pages of the form,
write your initials, find papers – you also
notice in the postures of her colleagues.
'What's wrong? *Something* is… forgive me for prying.'
'Oh, it's just we've worked so hard
to increase client satisfaction – see the new lighting?
But this administration
only wants privatization.
We'll be gone in a month, some company's taking over.'
'That's awful,' you say, with the emotion
one feels around a girl about to cry.
(She doesn't.) 'What will you do?' 'I'll have to
go back to Montana and shear sheep
with my father. The others…'
Your anger grows. 'And you'll all be replaced by machines,
and the rates and fees will skyrocket
in the name of savings and efficiency.'
'It's worse than that,' says a supervisor
who has been slowly approaching
behind the counter, rallying rather than browbeating
her troops, and who now stops by Athena.

MARY (thus her nametag),
middle-aged, plainly dressed,
projects brains and motherliness.
She remarks how it appears there's
no public any more, no public interest;
there are only stakeholders
and who counts as one is decided by
the rich. You feel you could talk with her,
unhurried, until
a new socioeconomic order
dawned; and her presence seems to hearten
Athena. But by now having reached
the last page of the form, you sign your name, fish out
your Mastercard. The fee
is exorbitant, unprecedented,
but vaguely you think it will help *them*,
the girl, the woman… Later
you do some checking. Insofar
as data is available, you learn
the place was privatized the month before.

Romance of the Pen

'Would it surprise you that, somewhere
out there, a man is writing about us
with no attempt to mimic our curt,
brutal, slang- and acronym-laden,
coldly pragmatic patois? Or to reflect
the distinctions that in our experience
loom largest: between guards and cons,
black and white, virility/passivity,
number and type of outside contacts,
or even length of sentence?
What would you say of such a man?'
'I'd say he's a fool. However,
his existence wouldn't surprise me, since fools
predominate. I'd only wonder why he does it.'
'Well, that's the question. You'll notice
he has bestowed on us
his patois (which he wouldn't regard as such),
though one suspects he's aware
it wouldn't flourish here.' 'Does he at least
respect our insistence on the word 'con,' our fierce
rejection of 'prisoner'?' 'He does.
Which indicates some research on his part.'
'Perhaps – assuming racial difference –
he's a racist, believes his discourse
superior to ours, and pursues an effect
like that of a minstrel show.'
'That's possible, but I think there's more to it...
He's afraid.' 'If he were here,
I'd give him something to fear!'
'In a sense he already is.
Which isn't to say he would ever indulge
that common stylistic habit
of likening whatever minor problem
of the self to catastrophes like ours
so that one's own becomes the only pain.

Simply, we are a passing metaphor
for him of isolation and entrapment.'
'It sounds as though you're half in love
with this 'work.' You're entirely too forgiving!'
'Not at all. What's lacking is the least hint
of compassion. For us. To be fair, however –
and I suppose one must be fair –
we'd likely reject (would we not?)
any sympathy he showed;
mistrust it, wonder what his angle was;
and the more detailed and realistic
the presentation, the more we would complain.
Which may be closer to his deeper point.'
'How does it end, this piece?'
'I'm not sure. I suspect with a cadence
ever-popular in those circles,
the toneless abstracted fadeout.'

Expedition

When the fact of peak oil began to seep,
as these things do, through mental
cinderblocks, people bought SUVs.
This reference may seem adventitious,
but isn't. A particularly fat one
sped round a corner. A boy (quite young,
I can't tell ages) was running toward
that curb. He appeared to be seeing
some lovely commodity or destiny.
And stopped, inches from
the car, which raced on.
The father (had he lost control?
been distracted?) ran up and berated/
embraced him (the phrases and reasoning
came I thought from the mother)
and pulled him crying away. But what struck me
was the kid's expression, stopping –
pudgy arms wide, eyes wide with sudden complete
disillusionment. (And the fact that,
though part of a system, he did stop.)

So to Speak

I am, so to speak, the hero
of a Beat-era novel its author
would have loved to see called existential.
It isn't bad or good. It wears
its influences lightly; so do I.
At the end I don't die – from an overdose,
cirrhosis (which might have come later), being shot by
the crazed self-identified Trotskyist
from Part Two, or the girl I treated badly
(she went back to Dublin).
I can say with some pride that I have
no last vision of suburbs, employment,
or a compensatory son;
things simply fade out, I fade,
which appears to be why I'm immortal.
We get together, we remaindered
heroes, at the Blue Note and Five Spot.
Those who are neither women,
black, gay, or Jews, and especially those
who were never optioned for movies, keep a low profile.
We talk about the news, your news,
which – I know you can't see this –
is incredibly, off-Broadway funny.
(We ourselves remain protected
by the Strategic Air Command.)
My place in the East Village
is still thirty bucks a month.
I sail for weeks to Dublin
by freighter to apologize again.
You may wonder if we get bored. But to
be bored you have to be alive, and I,
according to the reviewer(s), wasn't.
I can mourn though, and sometimes
on bad nights I seek out my author's flat.
He was neat. His pens still lie in a row.

I dust the Anglepoise lamp, put Art Tatum
and Bird on the stereo.
His ghost never shows, but I do.

Afternoon

The afternoon drags. Contemplation
is a worn, faded chair
identical, they say, to those
in the anterooms of action.
Doors open. Important people,
exiting, defer
to people pretending to be important.
Inevitably, power and pretense
are what one contemplates, waiting
to be noticed, wanting but having made
no effort to be noticed. Or important.

The least tremor, loss of focus, or
indiscipline could transpose one
to a clinic. – Windows there
are not distinct elements;
reveal nothing, despite accumulated
eons of patient gaze.
One's tablet only confirms
the message of old wounded magazines:
A seed drifts, and if it isn't
pecked and doesn't land
in fire, rock, or water, thinks itself clever.

– Or to a courtroom. –
Here too the fantasy of the accused
is to change bodies
with witnesses or onlookers, forever happier;
such metamorphosis is what they fear.
Guards self-incarnate in sidearms;
the innocent, more tenuously,
in innocence, to stop the drift. Until
at the never-comfortable close
of day, one's name is called,
truth mentioned, and one rises and is seen.

Hoot

Was it, I wonder, a good idea
to have both Food and Book Fairs
at the same time in the same few cordoned blocks?
Won't the odors – exotic, organic,
mostly vegetable (the blood-scent of broccoli,
the bile of roasted Brussels sprouts)
yet coexisting sweetly with satay –
suffuse pages and bindings?
Or is the *delicious book*
the Fair's intended memento, even in fact
its theme? People swarm
both sets of booths, their colours, clothes, and genders
as various and vivid
as gourds and peppers or the covers
of offerings from university presses.
The young wear the new limb
that texts while the hard-wired ones embrace.
Love, outreach rule. Even I,
with my studied Baudelairean detachment
or act, may be viewed as included.

Only beyond the sawhorses
and yellow tape at the ends of the Fair
are the greys visible. They stand
in fields of something that isn't wheat,
beside buildings whose ugliness
they love as they love their own. It isn't fair
to call them zombies. They have the vitality
of chemicals or magnets; simply,
variety all looks the same to them.
Sometimes one breaks the line, runs in
and shoots a few of us, but he too evidently
seeks, more than serves, death.
That will change; hence my diffidence.
I retreat and browse the books.
So many of them lately – all, in a way –
insist that we should *listen*
to those who can't.
Wouldn't it be (I reflect) a hoot
if, when the greys charge,
they burn the lot of them as well as us?

Huge

Though I'm sure you'd deny it, you never think
a ridiculous/exotic
person like me thinks. But as the crowd
we strenuously gathered surges toward
the line we have drawn and is beaten back
with long sticks (our culture values
physical contact), I think
I'm clever: that line is far behind
the one they will eventually flow to,
which can be held. I suggested this
to my chief; it isn't clear
if I'm favored or being punished, stationed here.
Now, for hours, a lull. I think:
my salary is X; the informal
protections I offer, 2X. Official expenses,
including my family (managed
as austerely as possible), .9X;
unofficial, 1.5. You see that, like you,
like everyone in the world,
I struggle to make ends meet.
That's what I think about, sternly assessing
the crowd (which smells as bad to me
as I would to you) for anomalies
of tribe or sect or tint, whether actually dangerous
or dangerous on principle. And suddenly
they surge, wave flags and cheer as we hold
or beat them back, and you pass
in your motorcade. You wave; I see you
two meters away, like a fierce
but pampered golden dog. Our eyes meet,
and I sense how hot it must seem
to you, outside the car,
and how hard it is among
your fleeting flushed expressions
to choose the right one. And I straighten

my uniform and posture and
am proud in my small way
to share with you the duty
of keeping the world safe.

Acknowledgements

Thanks are due to the editors of the following publications, where some of these poems first appeared: *Adelaide Literary Magazine, The Alarmist, Blackbox / Manifold, December, Cacti, Dream Monocle, East Coast Literary Review, The Gap Toothed Madness, The Lake, Masque & Spectacle, Modern Poetry Quarterly Review, New Bourgeois, North Chicago Review, Occupoetry, Rat's Ass Review, Razor, The Stray, Survision Magazine, Tenement Block Review, The Valley Review, Verse-Virtual* and *Visitant*.